Why MacOS? Why a Mac?
A (somehow unusual) Handbook for MacOS

Leonard Lowe

2017-10-18

The Book

A lot of talk these days is about the Macintosh and Apple. With their mobile devises like iPhone and iPad, Apple became the most valuable brand in the world. And not without a cause: they are just brillant.

But is this also true for their much older product: the Macintosh Computer that is around since ancient 1984.

Compared to the mainstream, Apple always used to be a different world, and many elaborate computer users think about – and doubt – whether to switch to the Mac or not. Wasn't the Mac just for the creative people, for the people who weren't really power users? Is a Mac even a real computer? Or is it just some nice point-and-click thing, that lacks depth and complexity?

This is where this book comes in: it tells you in a different way than all the others what the Mac is and what it will do for you. It tells you from a historical perspective, shows its development and what each step brought for the user.

This book will tell you exactly what advantages a Mac has compared to the other competitors, like Windows or Linux. And it will tell you which of the many myths and rumors around it are true – and which aren't.

The Author

Leonard Lowe is an engineer, scientific researcher and professor for mechanical engineering. Throughout his career his success formula was always 'never believe, always question – never stand still, always learn – never accept, always understand'.

He is the author of several books on technology, nature, philosophy, history and politics.

Beyond his professional live he is a tech and hi-tech enthusiast, computer geek, brillant thinker and writer. He loves to acquire knowledge and share it. His sharp analyses and unusual views help his readers making the right decisions in many different areas of life.

Online Book Stores

Books from THINK-eBooks are available at
http://think-ebooks.com/where-to-buy/

Imprint

Contents

0 Foreword — 9

1 The Grounds — 15

2 The Hardware — 23

3 Open Source Software — 29

4 10.0 Cheetah (2001) — 31
4.1 Unix 32
4.2 Model-View-Controller 34
4.3 Dock 36

5 10.1 Puma (2001) — 39

6 10.2 Jaguar (2002) — 41

7 10.3 Panther (2003) — 43
7.1 Expose 44

8 10.4 Tiger (2005) — 47
8.1 Spotlight 48

9 10.5 Leopard (2007) — 51
9.1 Time Machine 52
9.2 Spaces 54

10 10.6 Snow Leopard (2009)   **57**
10.1 Preview 58
10.2 Quicktime X 59

11 10.7 Lion (2011)   **61**
11.1 iCloud 63
11.2 App Store 65
11.3 Launchpad 68
11.4 Notes App 69
11.5 Autosave & Versions 72
11.6 Multi Touch 75

12 10.8 Mountain Lion (2012)   **77**
12.1 Fusion Drive 78
12.2 Power Nap 79
12.3 Dictation 80
12.4 Text-to-Speech 81

13 10.9 Maverics (2013)   **83**
13.1 Finder Tags 84

14 10.10 Yosemite (2014)   **87**
14.1 Maildrop 88
14.2 iPhone Calls 89

15 10.11 El Capitan (2015)   **91**
15.1 iCloud Drive 92

16 10.12 Sierra (2016)   **95**
16.1 Siri 96
16.2 Universal Clipboard 97
16.3 Optimized Storage 98

17 10.13 High Sierra (2017)   **103**

18 What I Still Miss   **105**

19 The Author 111

20 Just One More Thing. . . 115

21 Recommendations 119

Chapter 0

Foreword

What you get with Mac OS is just one thing: Killer Features galore. And all these in perfect shape and condition, (nearly) without any bugs and running fast and seamless like crazy.

That's just the short version, here is the long one: Since 2001, when Apple merged the old Mac OS 8 with its paradigm of easy access and transparency with the technologically superior NeXT System from Steve Jobs second installment, the NeXT corp., Apple's Mac OS is basically a NeXT system with the Apple Mac desktop on top. It looks basically the same as previous versions, it is used the same way, but under the hood everything changed – to be even better.

You cannot overestimate the importance of the technology behind the NeXT system. It is not only built with state of the art object oriented design patterns, it also is written in Objective-C a variation of the C language that is still very very fast like C but at the same time offers the bug-proof and elegant techniques of object oriented programming.

This killer combination makes OS-X fail-save, rugged and blazingly fast at the same time. And it is so compact that Apple was able to port it into a tiny portable device, they called the iPhone (a mobile pocket computer Steve sold us being a telephone). And also on this plattform OS-X (now called iOS) runs like crazy.

But there is more than technology. OS-X is more than other

systems oriented towards the user. Nothing is in your way. One major issue with other systems like Windows or Linux Deskops is that the software seems to be more important than you (the user) are.

Like in the (very) old days, the person in front of the computer is considered the administrator of that computer. His main purpose is to care for the computer and do everything that it is able to run. Somehow this image of the user as being primarly the admin of the PC transferred itself to this very day in the way Windows and Linux approach their users.

If such an old fashioned application or a system service thinks it could place a message right in front of you – no matter what – and you have to answer it *right now* it does so. The software seems to have priority 1 and then, when the software is satisfied, your intentions come second. Often these systems want attention from you to install or update software, antivirus updates and that on a daily basis. When I still used Windows I knew that my first 10 or so clicks on the mouse would be to satisfy the system and those components, like the Acrobat Reader that sometimes wanted to update every freakin day.

But this is not the image the user has in the Apple philosophy. Not so in Mac OS.

Completely not so. Even if the system just runs a backup or updates something, you normally can even shutdown the whole system or logout from your user without 1) being held up by the system and even more important 2) without damaging the system and having it not start or bombard you with error messages next time round.

And on Mac OS you don't even need an Antivirus software anyway, because nobody managed to write any kind of virus for it till this very day. (with the exception of Microsoft Office Trojans, of course, that MS Office manages to bring to the Mac).

No app is allowed to interrupt the user. And of course not with ads or unnecessary things. When you start a Mac it is at your service not the other way around.

When you today buy a Windows PC you get so much software

with it, that the system is nearly unusable. With the Mac only comes software from Apple and not one single trial software.

For more than 15 years now, Apple improves and develops this brillant system. And here is why it is even better than that:

OS-X has a lot of functions built in that you need additional third party software for in other systems – if they even exist. And this bonus software is not like other apps of that kind worth what they cost. This software is really really good! Crucial functions, important functions, system-relevant functions are covered that way, like... but that's obviously what we talk about in this book.

In this book we deconstruct what was added to Mac OS over the years. This automatically results in a logical understanding how some of the services and apps came to the system and for what purpose.

Naturally we're not talking about all the features of OS-X. You certainly know what windows and the Dock are and what they are used for. What this book will point out are the not so obvious gems of OS-X that perhaps also help the decision whether to move from another system to the Mac (or not).

If you understand the evolution of something, you more deeply understand its use and purpose and what it was meant for in the first place. If you understand the history of things, you are able to understand them on a different level, in a different dimension: time.

Not only for the Crazy Ones

This book is for everyone who thinks about switching over to the Mac but is not quite sure if this is a good idea. At least a step of that magnitude means a lot of change and it takes some effort to undergo that change. Nothing's without a price.

This book will give you informations about features and reasons why in the eyes of the author, the Mac is a brillant system that is very much worth the extra money Apple charges for their systems – and the extra mile to go to move over to it. Simply put: you will get any penny back in form of quality, usability and relaxed working.

But this book is also for the Mac user who wants to learn more about his system and its origins and functions.

Because if there is any weakness in Apple's way of doing things, it's that they do not document their features well. Indeed Mac OS has a lot of very powerful features that don't get used to their full potential, either because Apple does not use them a lot themselves in their own apps, or because nobody seems to understand the scheer power that lies within them. The tagging of files on file system level is such an example.

And that way, this book might help also the experienced Apple user to find out features and possibilities to use their Mac they always were looking for, but were afraid to ask.

Features to Cover

There are three classes of features in Mac OS that will be covered in this book: the big killer features and killer Apps that are shipped with the system or as part of the formerly called iLife and iWork software packages that are today mostly free or very cheap and secondly the many small refinements that made the system apps of Mac OS like Finder, Safari and Mail better and better over the years and third of course the system functions of Mac OS that make so many easy and genius ways to work with the system even possible.

Is the Author a Fanboy?

Don't get me wrong: I am *not* a fanboy (of course not, who wants to be called that anyway?). I don't recommend all that I am writing about in order to feel connected to something more significant and bigger than I feel myself. I solely recommend this, because I can see the major difference between this system and the other competing ones and I really like helping you making these advantages work also for you.

Am I payed by Apple?

No, unfortunately not.

Take Care! Yours,
Leon Lowe in June 2017

Chapter 1

The Grounds

Here's to the Crazy Ones

Here's the most beautiful Ad of all Time: and it shows the ideology, the philosophy, the attitude and the sheer intelligence, how Apple sees their products and their customers nailed on the head. They say it exactly in the See Things Different ad campaign for the Mac:

> »Here's to the crazy ones. The misfits. The rebels. The troublemakers. The round pegs in the square holes. The ones who see things differently.
>
> They're not fond of rules. And they have no respect for the status quo. You can quote them, disagree with them, glorify or vilify them. About the only thing you can't do is ignore them.
>
> Because they change things. They push the human race forward. While some may see them as the crazy ones, we see genius.
>
> Because the people who are crazy enough to think they can change the world, are the ones who do.«

This is the text spoken to the ad that shows a lot of famous persons all standing out because they swam against the tide: Einstein, Martin Luther King, and many others.

Figure 1.1: Think different Commercial

And to be honest: this text, this is Steve Jobs about Steve Jobs. These computers are built for people like him. Crazy ones. Geniuses. People who don't want neither limits nor rules but brillant and painless tools to work with.

Where des the name come from

Well, talk is cheap, right? No, it's not. At least not always.

Is it now OS-x or OS-ten? Well, it's both. Both ways totally make sense and here is why. Of course the literal genius connection is that in latin numbers X means ten. But there is more: It is OS-x because it is a Unix kind system. And traditionally Unix systems have that x in their name, like Solaris... no, just joking. But like Linux, NeXT, HP-UX, Minix, Ultrix, Sinix, Xenix (even has two!), AIX and of course the family name *Unix* itself. The graphical user interface standard for Unix systems is called X-Window system. Enough to make that point?

And the ten? Of course the real last full version of Mac OS before OS-X was Mac OS 8. Mac OS 9 was somehow a transitional product for the migration to OS-X.

The Tic-Toc strategy

Everybody knows that you need roundabout three versions of a software to work properly and fast. V1: you write the code and make it work. V2 you have some improvements to make it consistent and bug free. V3 you remove all code that is unnecessary and even replace some parts with better and faster algorithms.

So if you just add and add more and more functions to your software, you end up with a huge system with a lot of half working and slow functions. You need the steps to consolidate your system and optimize your function without adding new features in the first place.

This strategy is called Tic-Toc strategy and is also used in other fields, like e.g. microprocessor development.

In a Tic phase you add new features and in a Toc-phase you consolidate and optimize them. So the Tic product is always that with a lot of new features, while the Toc product has not a lot of new things, but is faster and more stable in every aspect.

Snow Leopard (note the name) is one of those refined versions: it's a better Leopard. The names reflect that. And because it is Apple this one is of course a white Leopard.

Probably the cat names should reflect that OS-X runs smooth, quick, refined and elegant like a cat – and probably is as deadly to their opponents as these killer cats are. Think about it:

Steve loved these symbolisms. When he left the Apple offices in 1983 with a team of some loyal colleagues to built his visionary project, the Macintosh, they indeed raised a pirates flag from their new building to show everyone that they were kind of outlaws, because they intended to make this new computer against the will of the rest of the Apple board. And, boy, was he right.

So probably also the cats have their hidden meaning. And of course they reflect the Tic Toc strategy.

But this wasn't so from the start. The first OS-X had the codename 'Cheetah'. The fastest land animal on the planet. This was probably meant to say, it's fast! Which it wasn't. It was Version 1.0 for goodness sake. What would you expect?

And then the following cats were just other cats, like 10.1 Puma, 10.2 Jaguar, 10.3 Panther and 10.4 Tiger. These just have no clever relation to each other. Pumas are the small moutain lions of North America. Jaguars are the Leopards of South America. Panthers are basically Leopards with black on black fur. And Tigers are the large cats of Asia. No real structure there, or... is there? If you look closely, they get increasingly bigger. Pumas are more like big cats, also Jaguars are rather small, Panthers are bigger, like Leopards, nearly as big as Lions, and Tigers, boy! they are the biggest predators of them all. So OS-X got bigger and bigger, hu?

Then from Leopard on, things became more structured and planful. All went towards the 'Lion', the King of all the Animals.

Very obvious is this is in the relations of 10.5 Leopard to 10.6 Snow Leopard, 10.7 Lion to 10.8 Mountain Lion and 10.12 Sierra to 10.13 High Sierra Less obvious but still recognizable is this in 10.10 Yosemite to 10.11 El Capitan, as El Capitan is a big mountain in Yosemite Natl. Park. With 10.9 Maverics they obviously were on a name path that lead to nothing.

So Much of Anything

The Mac in fact today has so many solutions, concepts, ideas and shortcuts built in that often you take the long way because you just don't know about the genius shortcut. Sometimes users don't even try something because they believe it will not work – basically because they know from other systems like Linux or Windows that it dosen't work. Truth is: on the Mac a lot of those limits we all accepted over the years don't exist or got a seamless and elegant workaround, that they actually don't exist for Mac users.

Think about it: from 2000 on, when OS-X began to materialize, every year 100 to 200 new functions had been implemented which are alone the unbelievable number of about 1700 to over 3500 functions, most of them still inside Mac OS and available to take advantage of. And these are only the ones that the user is able to, well, use. Like manage his system Fonts, make phone call from the Mac, use Windows based networks like so, write emails with more than 1 GB of attachments to any other user on the web, share his information from Calender, Contacts, Reminders, etc. with other users, collaborate on files together at the same time, have video phone calls like you know from scifi movies, send a route from Maps directly with just one click to you iPhone to use it there for turn-by-turn directions, copy a text or a image on your iPad and a second later paste it on your Mac, and so on and on and on.

This book will recapitulate, what functions are there for you to use. Because if Apple is really bad on something, it is telling users, what their software is really capable of. But that's ok, that's what you have me for.

Unobtrusiveness

Every new feature in Mac OS is integrated seamless, almost unnoticable. Often one single new button or icon is all you see of it, if you don't look for it. Apple does not make you use a new feature by let's say activating it from the start and giving you no other opportunity than to use it. Apple does not tell you what to do. It's the other way around: often you don't even recognize new features until you suddenly find out that they are there.

That has a very precious effect: every new Mac OS version you install and use, looks pretty much exactly the same as the previous one. At first you are disappointed, because you expected something spectacular, something new, something mind blowing. But soon you find out that nothing is more disturbing in everyday work, than things that are spectacular, new and mind blowing. Work efficiency relies on continuity and that begins with a not too heavily changing work environment.

That way you feel at home immediately on every new release of Mac OS. Everything is where it used to be and where it is supposed to be, you can just continue working where you left off, as if nothing happened at all.

But some features you stumble across and you find out that this is now possible and helps a lot, or sometimes you ask yourself if this is new or has ever been there without you noticing.

The downside of this philosophy is of course that it sometimes takes you a while to find that very useful new feature, because Apple does not urge you to recognize it.

Other features that add massively to your advantage, like, say, Time Machine for safety, Spotlight for finding things or the App Sore for convenient app installation and updating are of course activated from the start and offer you their services, but even those are mainly working in the background a lot without you usually noticing.

But don't misunderstand me. If you, for some odd reason, do not want them, you can also turn them off. A Mac serves you and your needs, not the other way around.

Bugs: Trust them, they'll fix it

When I think about bugs, there is something else that comes to my mind that I constantly recognize with Apple products. The bugs get fixed.

This sounds like the most natural thing of all. Arn't bugs there to be fixed? Of course. But in the reality of the software world there is a lot of software around where this isn't done at all. Even major software packages from major suppliers sport the same bugs sometimes over years. Even critical ones. Just recently a major bug was found in the Linux encryption package that made all the encryption ineffective if you knew how to exploit it. This bug was there unnoticed and unfixed for over 10 years. Can you imagine what this means for the security of systems that rely on that module?

Not so with Apple. If there is one thing you notice about Apple and bugs is that they get away nearly as quickly as you encounter them. Meaning: if you find something that works odd or does not quite as expected, runs in timeouts or something like that: just have trust. With the next update release this behavior with a high probability of over 90% will be fixed and gone.

But sometimes this isn't the case. Something doesn't really work as expected but the updated doesn't change that. And that often means that what you encounter might not be a bug at all.

See, Mac apps have a strange behavior: they have config files they manage themselves. And these config files, over the years of their existence (because with every update, you entire configuration is preserved of course, and so are the configuration files) might contain configurations that somehow don't work properly anymore.

I have such a problem of that magnitude in Finder: when I copy files by dragging and dropping since my last Mac OS update I don't get this green bubble with the plus sign in it any more that tells me that Finder is going to copy the files instead of moving them. This is such an odd behavior I am talking about. And it is not a real bug, but probably based in something in the Finder config file that does not stand the test of time anymore.

So what to do? Easy. These config files are a bit like magic also. If you just delete them, every app writes a new default config file. And then the app usually runs as expected (with the exception that your special configuration wished, of course, are gone, you just deleted them).

In other systems, deleting or damaging or even changing a config file means that the app probably won't start any more, complain a lot or will crash early. Not so in Mac OS. You can delete every config file you want, the app or even the system will just write a new one to work with.

Using Macs Over the Years

PCs get slower with every new version of Windows. There are new features and these take computing power, right? There is no way around that fact.

Well, not so with the Mac. Of course also here new features take away computing power. But Apple at the same time is constantly inventing new technological tweaks that compensate for that. That way, the battery time of the Macbooks increased more and more, instead of getting shorter and shorter. That same way, battery time for every iPad is at least 10 hours. Since the very first one. And that despite the fact that iPads are today several hundred times faster than this first one.

That is partly owed to the power saving technologies of the Intel CPUs and chipsets, but also to the hord of features Apple implements to fight power consumption. That way, hugely faster Macbooks with unbelievably brillant displays today run longer and way faster than their old slower duller ancestors.

The same on the desktop. You may install the newest Mac OS on rather old machines, like back from 2010. Today, in 2017 a.D., still Macs from 2010 are supported by the latest Mac OS Version. And don't get me wrong: not in slow motion, but fast and smooth.

That are computers that are today over 7 years old! A huge timespan in an industry that used to double its computing power every 18 months. It basically means that you may run the latest OS-X system on hardware that..., let's do some quick math: let's say 7 years divided by 18 months, this is roughly 4 cycles of doubling computing power. That means x2 x2 x2 x2 = 16 times. You may run today's OS-X on a system that is expected to be 16 times (!) slower than a modern Mac. But it runs beautifully even on that machine!

This says a lot about what you get back from the raw power of the hardware you bought. If you think about that from the other way around, it means that with every new release of Mac OS, the Mac indeed gets a bit faster or at least stays the same from the users point of view – despite new features and possibilities, due to all the new features that indeed makes the Mac even more effective.

Chapter 2

The Hardware

Ok, I won't start with that old word Steve Jobs repeated quoting:

>»People who love their software need to make their own
> hardware«

Well... I just did. So now, how is Apple hardware? It's fast. So much for that. Isn't that sufficient? No, it isn't.

Beauty

And even if you deem that being not so overly important: Apple hardware is beautiful, made from simple and great materials. Why might that be not so important? Because it is a tool, right. A computer is made to do things not to be looked at. It doesn't matter if it is made from cheap plastic or beautify brushed aluminum, it doesn't matter if the touchpad is made from rubber or glas, right?

Well, I don't think so. It is the same with all the things you surround yourself, you use and touch: it gives you a feeling of who you are. If you are constantly surrounded by cheap things, you over time begin to feel cheap yourself. You standards drop. You more and more become what you are surrounded with. You adapt to your environment.

If you surround yourself with high quality things, things that feel great when you touch them, even look great when you see

Figure 2.1: iMac with Aluminum Body (this isn't just the display, it's the whole computer)

them, it also tells you, who you are and you adapt to that. It sets the tone, it is one piece of information about who you are – and who you want to be, what your vision is of yourself. And if you surround yourself with things of beauty that becomes your style of doing things yourself – with a sense for beauty.

So in my opinion: it makes a difference if your computer hardware is a loud, cheap, ugly blob of some matter or some beautifully crafted aluminum case with glas and steel parts. It sets a tone.

Silence

But what's more important than that is: silence! Apple hardware is silent.

Let's be completely honest about that. I am a power user, but todays computing power is much more than I need. The times are over when you needed the newest Intel processor (sorry Intel) to be happy and it made a big performance difference if you had a i386-33 or a i486-66. Today we are not talking 33 MHz, but a hundred times more: 3 GHz. And today I don't even know how many GHz my processors do. Ok. Just found out my old Macbook Pro (made in 2010, that is 7 years old!) I am writing on this morning has 2.4 GHz. What the heck do I care? It is blazingly fast – esp. since I replaced the old Apple harddisk with a SSD.

So in this day and age it is more the other way around. What you really need is three things: lots of memory, a SSD and... silence. The quality of your work environment depends more on silence than anything else. If your computer sounds like a Boeing 747 at takeoff, you cannot work without being utterly disturbed by the noise. Your creativity and your knowledge and your joy of working can only unfold when you have silence and peace around you - so your focus on what matters is not disturbed. And silence means no fan movement – and fans move when they need to blow out heat – and heat comes from... too much computing power. So what you need today is not the most expensive, most powerful Intel processor – but the other way around: the least powerful one.

So I bought the least powerful iMac to be even more silent. And I can say after 3 years of daily use: I was completely right. I never ever experienced just even a slight lack of power, not at writing (of course not), but also not at editing images and fotos, not at cutting HD video with iMovie. What more would I want?

And one thing I meanwhile experience every day... come, listen yourself... it is... nearly... completely... still. It just sounds like... it's off. But it isn't. It's running. You can see it. The display is on. Isn't that beautiful?

That is a Mac. It is silently looking good, while doing all the work that you shouldn't do.

A Cheap Copy

How about a Hackintosh? Doesn't that deliver better performance at a lower price? Like a Mac Pro workstation performance for a cheap PC pricetag? Since Mac OS is running on Intel plattforms, this became an option. And isn't that the best of both worlds?

No it isn't. Don't dare! Don't even try! Just don't! That way you don't get a Mac. Even if the thing runs OS-X. Here is why:

You must understand what you buy with a Mac. You don't buy a piece of hardware, you don't buy a tool, you buy peace of mind. That is the thing at the core. You buy relaxation. You buy a machine that does so many things by itself without bothering you, that you can relax and concentrate on your work. Because you know, everything the Mac does without you noticing will be all right. That is: down to the very basic things of all day computer usage: like saving files – what the Mac does for you. Or opening your apps. Or opening the last files you worked with. Things like that and many many others.

When you finally got rid of your psychosis of worrying what might go wrong next, a sickness that Windows has trained you over the years, you finally know it: the Mac won't crash, the Mac won't swallow your work, the Mac won't get on your nerves any time soon, with little requesters like you know them from the other systems: "Error 3572: Error." The Mac won't do anything like that at all.

And that phenomenon depends on the stability and reliability of the system as a whole. If you take that away by building you own hardware that might be not perfectly compatible, you take everything away the Mac is all about. In that sense: a Hackintosh isn't a Mac even if it runs OS-X. It is just another PC.

Of course you can install Mac OS on some more or less compatible PC hardware. On the internet there are sites that analyze which mainboards, graphics cards, Wifi, Thunderbolt, Bluetooth etc. components are used in which Mac and of course you can purchase these (with the risk of getting the same or another slightly not so compatible revision), you can built such a machine by yourself and start it up.

Have you ever opened the case of a Mac? I did. And I was astonished. There is only very little typical PC hardware in it. Everything is tightly stuffed and arranged and put ontop of each other – that's why Macs are so small. There are even connectors that are obviously designed to save space so you literally need a tweezer to plug it in.

A Mac isn't a PC at all. It is hardware made with a lot attention to detail. And that's why it is more expensive than standard PC hardware.

But what do you get with a Hackintosh? You get a PC in a probably ugly huge case, with a loud PC fan as it isn't at any rate optimized, you will experience a lack of features, like the built in camera, like the built in speakers etc.

But what is worse: until it runs, let's say, 95% of the time quite ok, you will have to fiddle around with drivers and kernel modules, restart it again and agin, just to see it crash again, and try and try and just experience errors and crashes.

Then you will have to read on the internet about workarounds and try some more and... it probably still crashes. Perhaps more seldom or just once a day. But you still have that feeling that any time soon something could dramatically go wrong with your computer – and with the work you to.

You get the idea. It will take you days up to weeks until you get a system that doesn't crash so often. But it probably still will. So what have you won, saving a few bucks?

The Mac is about relaxation and focus on your work and your results. The Mac is not about the Mac, it is about you.

If you built a Hackintosh you just take this most important thing away. You move the computer back into the center of your attention, you make the tool the purpose. And at the same time you move your focus away from you and away from the results of your work. In that sense a Hackintosh isn't any better than a Linux box or a Windows PC. They all use up too much of your energy.

With a Hackintosh you save some money buying the cheaper

PC hardware, but you give the most important thing away: peace of mind. And focus on you.

So just don't.

Chapter 3

Open Source Software

The open source software 'market' is as bottomless as it is often worthless. Amateur programmers of very different skills and experience levels do their best with very mixed results. So its pearls are often really buried under layers of mud and rubbish. But as Mac OS being a UNIX system at the core, it is not hard to port these tools to the Mac and so especially the pearls are available in Mac OS also and somehow also belong to the Mac's heritage, not just to Linux.

So there are the pearls and gems of open source community and some of them are even outstanding and a kind of must. Even if it is software that is not genuinely conceived for the Mac and often does not meet its user interface rules, some of these still are great pieces of software that make your day easier. Even if at first you probably have to consult the documentation files until you get things up and running. I would recommend to have a closer look at these:

LaTeX without question is the most flexible and professional text system there is. I write all my books in LaTeX. Even if the approach has a slightly steeper learning curve than the normal WYSIWYG writing app like Word and Pages, the flexibility and the result you get is worth the extra effort.

Pandoc   If I say command line, most Mac users will bounce back to another chapter. But still this is the most versatile tool when you want to convert text file formats. I for myself use it to convert LaTeX .tex files into .epub ebooks or plain text .txt files for different uses. It also can handle and convert various flavours of Markdown .md files. Very handy and worth the learning curve.

Graphviz   If you need flowcharts, tree charts and other visual illustrations, Graphviz is worth a look. Like LaTeX you in some sense 'program' or even 'code' your result what has an advantage and a disadvantage: the disadvantage obviously is that the apps accessibility has the charm of the pre-graphical-user-interface-1970s and is a bit bumpy at first. But the advantage of this approach is that you will never be as precise and clear what you want and get in any graphical user interface system. And precision is clearly perceived as being professional.

VLC   Sometime you don't want to first import an music album or an audio book into iTunes to listen to it. So you need another quick and easy player. To be honest, WinAMP still is a more flexible and to me better audio player than VLC, but for just occasional use it does its job ok.

VirtualBox   If you still need another OS, perhaps this is an app for you. Especially when you develop software that should also be tested on another OS, it's great to have it running in just another Mac Window. VirtualBox is the cheapest solution for that task and definitely worth a look.

Chapter 4

10.0 Cheetah (2001)

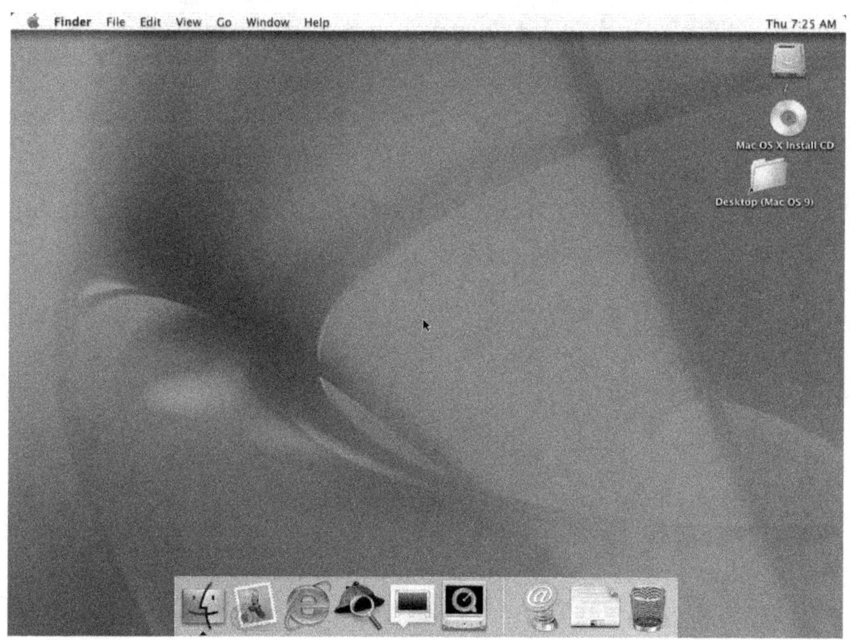

4.1   Unix

Mac OS X is a Unix based system

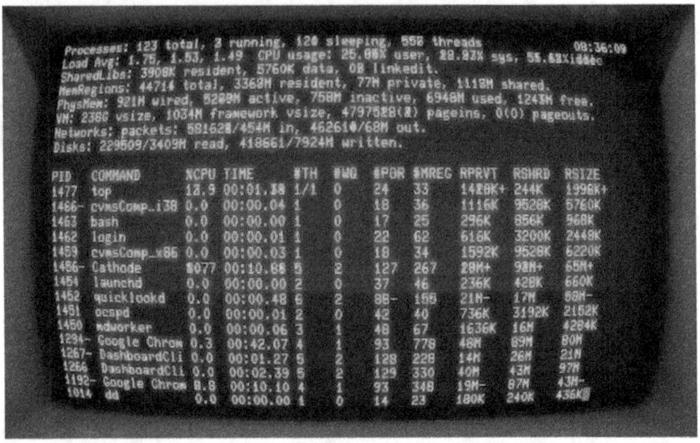

Figure 4.1: Typical Unix Terminal. Not exactly like the Mac at all...

Even if it doesn't look like that, Mac OS X is a Unix based system. And it is without question the best and most widely used Unix in the world. Why? Because today it runs on every Apple product. On every Mac, every iPhone, iPad and iPod, even every Apple TV and Apple Watch. And that says a lot. What then is Unix? Isn't that some old, whacky thing that runs on some black-and-white-text-terminal of strange servers from a by-gone era?

Well, yes and no. Unix is probably the most advanced OS in the world. It is continuously developed since 1969 at a lot of Universities in the US and all around the world. So there are a lot of core system features in Unix systems that are very elaborate, very well thought through, even academic, what in this context means very consistent and clever.

Unix always used to be the professional system for professionals. It had mechanisms like Multitasking and Memory Management long before Intel implemented those features in PC processors with the i386 family. So until the 1990s the hardware available to personal computing was just not able to run such sophisticated software. And not only for that reason, Unix hardware was about factor 10 times more expensive. A Sun Workstation did not cost $5,000 like a PC but $50,000. Way too much for the Home- and Personal Computer market.

But things changed. The power of the PC catched up and by the end of the century it overtook the old workstations. That was also the time Linux Torwalds began developing a Unix for PC hardware, he called Linux. Linux is a Unix, of course. And that way it was possible to use all that excellent and clever solutions of the Unix world finally with PC grade hardware.

And that way nearly every OS running today is more or less based on Unix, Unix ideas and Unix principles. With more or less success, as you can see in Linux and its mobile incarnation called Android.

In Mac OS that basically means that, like in any other Unix, the very foundations of the system are accessible through the terminal. And at that base Mac OS-X is very much like Unix. You can just use the Terminal of Mac OS-X like you would a Unix Terminal. With all the typical Unix shell commands, like ls, mv, cp, vi, with all the Unix tools, like rsync, nano, gcc, you may even work with shell scripts to control your Mac. You even may install 'homebrew', a project manager that offers you nearly every Linux package on the Terminal as a OS-X program. The OS-X core, called 'Darwin' is even available Open Source.

So at the core, OS-X has foundations that date back to 1969 and were developed ever since by the brightest minds of the computer world, not with revenue on their minds, but the genius of their solutions. And after 20 years of development in the 1990s this knowledge went into NeXTStep and some years later into the foundations of the first incarnation of OS-X.

Above that the Mac-typical stuff begins. The Mac Desktop. The Mac grade Desktop apps. But it is built on the most sophisticated and advanced foundation there is: Unix.

There is more to OS-X than just being a Unix. But it is one

piece of the puzzle, why it is so powerful.

4.2   Model-View-Controller

MVC: The Model-View-Controller OOP Design Pattern

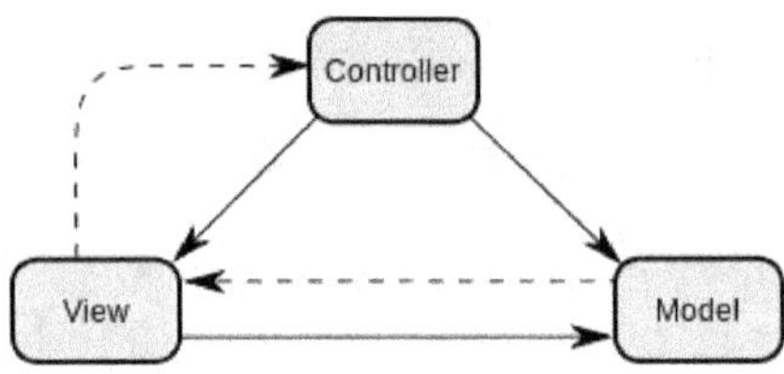

Figure 4.2: Model-View-Controller Design Pattern of Object Oriented Programming

MVC? What the heck might this kind of black magic be? Is this a * programmers manual? Why should I need to know this technical stuff in the first place? Isn't Apple all about keeping the user away from this cryptical tech stuff?

Well, indeed this is close to black magic. All design patterns are. But we're at the very beginning, thus at the very foundations, and because somehow all we're talking about is software some technical stuff helps to understand and appreciate all the other features better.

This basically means: the system isn't able to do all these fancy, luxurious, magical things we will talk about throughout the whole book, because some hard working genius programmer built all these things in, but, much more reliable and consistent, because the system is built like that. It is in its architecture, in its very genes and not one not-so-genius programmer can remove them by accident. They are always there, reliably.

And in order to understand what Mac OS is capable of – i.e. what you as a use can rely on – we just have a quick look at that technical basics before we go to the more user level things – that all by the way massively benefit from these very core features at the roots of Mac OS.

The Problem: In multi-tasking systems you often change things in one window and then switch to another window, to continue what you are up to.

But what is this: in the other window, nothing has changed. It's like: "Did... did I do something wrong? No. Or... What is going on...? Oh, yeah: click that reload button there, and... heck... yes, there it is. Uff, ok, everything's fine."

On conventional computers, i.e. with Windows or Linux on, this happens all the time. It happens so often that you got used to it. So used to it that you don't feel the pain that comes with it. But believe me: you suffer it, even if you don't notice any more. You feel the moment of doubt, of fear, something might have let your work of hours of hard work and pain disappear. With the MVC based Mac OS-X this ill fear is history.

The Solution: So let's start with saying what this MVC-OOP-*something* thing does: it makes that every change you make somewhere on the system, is immediately there, everywhere, where you would expect it, not only in the window you work with. No more 'Apply' buttons in the system settings, you flip the switch and it is already done.

Even better: you immediately see the result. Windows are updated immediately. If you change something in one app that is important for another app, like e.g. Finder (the File Manager of the Mac) it is already updated there even before you can go there to have look. No 'reload' buttons any more, no closing and re-opening windows, everything is always up-to-date. Always.

Just like in real life by the way: you also don't flip the lights on and then press some mysterious 'Apply' button, to execute it. The Mac feels more real live, less computer, more like a real device. Adding to this impression is the fact that the buttons flip immediately, no 'please wait...', no rotating something that tries

to tell you: wait, I'm not done reacting to one single button click!
– on a Mac you just 'click' and its done.

A little example: I some days ago updated my avatar image in
Contacts on my Mac. Accidentally on my iPhone also the Contacts
App was running. So I dropped my new foto to the appropriate
spot on the Mac, and 'bang' immediately the same picture was
updated on the iPhone. With less than a second delay. This is
MVC. This is close to magic.

This has its cause in the system structure and as well in programming language and environment of Mac OS: you cannot do it
differently – they won't let you. Already when you write code for
the Mac you are urged to use the MCV pattern. So not only the
system apps use this magic, and all the third party applications
fall short to that level of perfection. No, all the applications must
use the same mechanics, so they blend in and nothing disturbs
or blocks the perfectly running system with outdated bad written
code and freezing apps.

Design patterns of Object Oriented Programming were the
latest stuff in the early 1990s and are state of the art to this very
day. So of course the NeXT system, the system Mac OS-X is at the
core, made use of these latest fashion of computer programming.
And to this day, this pays off for the user.

4.3   Dock

Dock: Handy Cache, not necessarily an app-starter

At first you think the Dock is very basic. Even Windows had a
simple program-starter. But it isn't. It isn't a program-starter in
the first place. It is something much more flexible and advanced...

The Problem: There are many many many things stored on a
computer. Files and apps in insane quantities.

And some of them you use on a daily basis, some of them
sometimes and other near to never. If you look at these three

classes of apps and files you easily see that the number tenfolds in every class (at least).

You probably work with some 10 to 20 files every day, lists you keep, living documents you work with, projects you advance every day, necessary logs, ideas, notices, etc.

Then there are those files you sometimes use. Perhaps once a month or two or several times a year. Your tax documents, things you think about more seldom, but keep them alive. These are probably more 50 to 100 perhaps 200 files, depending on how long you work with the computer. In my case it is decades and you won't believe what stacks up in all this time.

And then there is the rest. Another 1000 to several thousand files that had been created someday, had their use, made sense but are forgotten. They lay around in directories and because they don't use enough space on the harddisk to be of any interest, they just stay there.

Basically, the 10 to 20 files you work with every day are somehow literally buried under these other several thousands of files. You cannot find them and if you do (e.g. using a well thought out directory structure or just Spotlight, it takes way too much time.

The same applies to apps.

The Solution: In the beginning the dock wasn't conceived as a program-starter like it is mostly used today. It was more meant as a cache for all kinds of documents, apps, links that you would be needing soon because you are actively working with them. For that reason, you can drag all kinds of stuff there, even if you probably don't (like me).

Of course the Dock became a handy app-starter and if you put directories in it, it is still a handy directory browser.

And it's very elegant and with a very small footprint. Its ability to stay outside the desktop area until you move the pointer to the bottom maximizes the area you have for your apps and the Magnification function helps you identify your icons even on smaller displays like on a laptop or an older computer.

A bit confusing is that the Dock is not the only app-starter tool on Mac OS. There is also the Launchpad presented later with 10.7 Lion in 2011 that is, to make things worse, a more consistent app starter tool than the Dock: it shows you *all* your apps, it is able to manage apps in *groups* and it uses the *whole screen* for you to select the app you want – and it works like its counterparts on the iOS devices, what makes it even more genius.

That stabilizes the Dock's role as a kind of shortcut cache for apps and files and not an app-starter in the first place.

And for that usage we (probably) all use it way too static: if I put an app in the Dock it usually stays there for a long time. The same applies to directories. And to be honest: I never put files in it. And that is probably the wrong way to use it.

Chapter 5

10.1 Puma (2001)

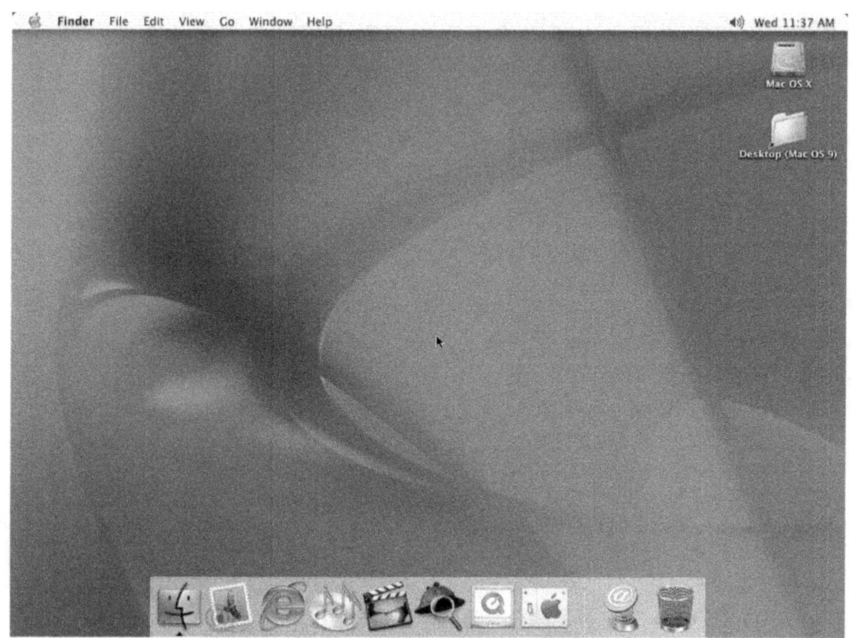

Chapter 6

10.2 Jaguar (2002)

Chapter 7

10.3 Panther (2003)

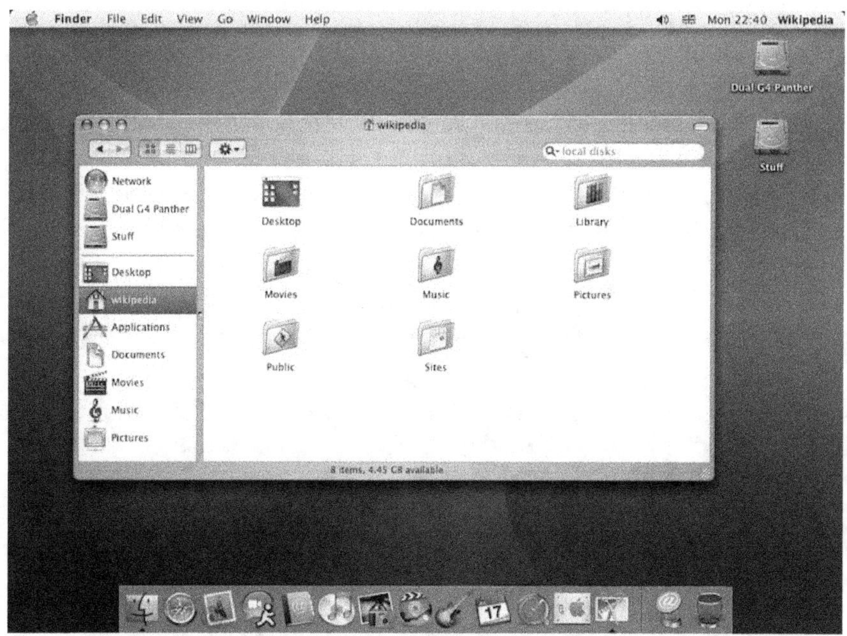

7.1   Expose

Expose: Full Screen Task Switcher

The Problem: On a multi-tasking system you tend to open a lot of applications at the same time, exchange data between them or just have them running in case you need them sometime.

When that case of using an app finally arrives, you want to have the app you need right in front of you, immediately. However, if you have, say, ten to twenty apps running, it might be not so easy to find the right app and the right window of that app. What to do? Search, click through all open windows? Or flip through it, like Windows offers you? No. You of course want to see all your options with one glance to choose as quickly as possible.

Figure 7.1: Desktop in Expose Mode

The Solution: Expose. Depending on what you prefer, you can start the app-overview function 'Expose' by clicking on an icon, using the F3 key on a Mac keyboard, with an elegant multitouch swipe down on the trackpad (my personal favourite), or by moving the mouse pointer to one edge of the desktop of your choice – or some other way you can think of.

Then smoothly all windows stacked on your desktop become small versions of themselves and the screen now shows all of them at the same time. You can choose which one you need, click on it and – voila – you have the app you want on top and can use it.

This same thing also works if you have some data glued to your mouse pointer. You can switch to expose, choose a window you want to drop the data into, let it come up and drop your stuff right in. Very easy. Very elegant.

From Mac OS-X 10.7 "Lion" in 2011 on Expose is called "Mission Control" because in this version it incorporates not only the overview of running apps and open documents, but also the management of Spaces (virtual desktops) as well as the (in my opinion highly useless) Dashboard all in one screen.

Chapter 8

10.4 Tiger (2005)

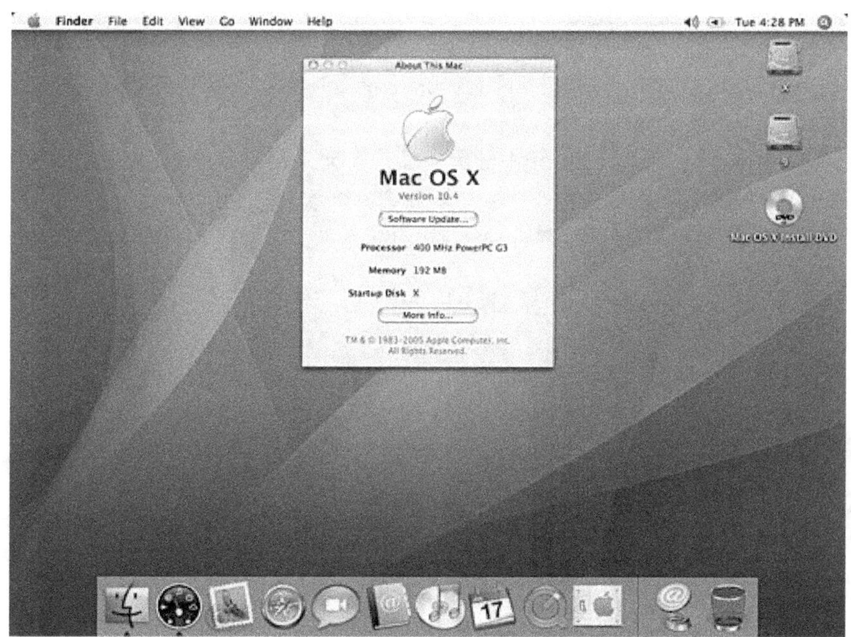

8.1   Spotlight

Spotlight: Local Search Engine for Your Files

The Problem: In these days of zero data loss due to systems like Time Machine, you over time, depending on your creativity and work ethics, have hundreds or thousands, even tens of thousands of files on your harddrive. Even elaborate directory structures make it hard to find the file you need.

Often you remember that you worked on a file, in the last few months or so, or you remember parts of the content of a file, but you simply cannot remember its name or where you put it. In all the directories it belongs to it is magically absent.

You wish, you had the Google Search on your desktop for just your files.

Well, you have. With Spotlight.

The Solution: With a keyboard stroke (command-space) you bring up your search field and then you might enter what you are looking for. The Spotlight engine will provide you with all the hits it can find.

The Spotlight index is not only filled with text files or spreadsheets. It also ready words and names in pdf files and other non-text file formats.

Furthermore the Spotlight engine is also used in apps, like iTunes, what makes search in these also blazingly fast and deeply integrated in the system.

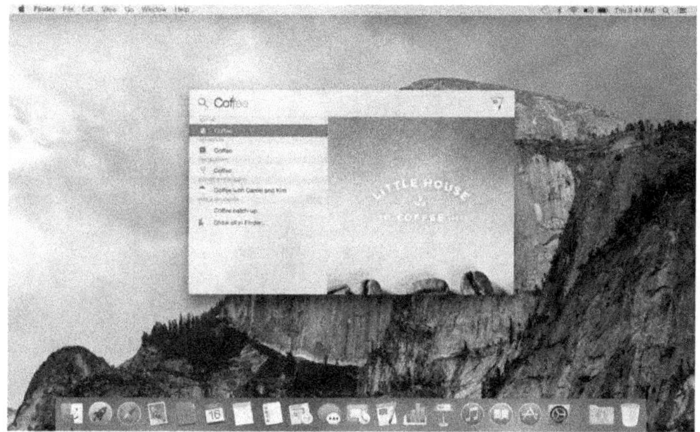

Figure 8.1: Spotlight Desktop Search Evolution in Mac OS 10.10 Yosemite

Chapter 9

10.5 Leopard (2007)

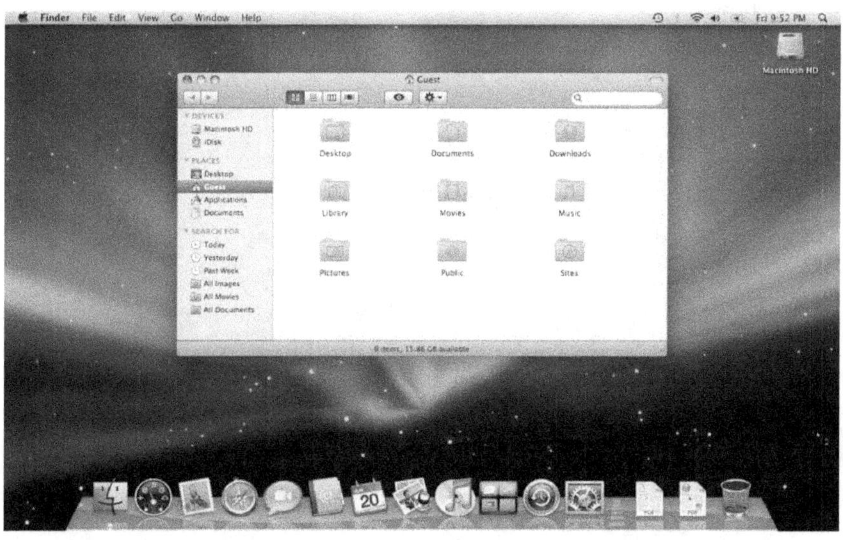

With Leopard and its successor Snow Leopard Mac OS shifted into third gear and became really grown up.

9.1   Time Machine

Time Machine: System Wide Backup System

Of course it is not a machine to travel through time. But it derives its name from its ability to move your Mac system back in time, esp. to the time before some error or crucial mistake occured and that way save all your files that eventually might be lost otherwise.

The Problem: Obviously computers don't run error-free. And of course not over years and decades. Failures will occur and threaten your files.

Even Mac OS-X is subjected to that fact. Data gets lost from time to time. It even might not be the OS's fault in the first place: a harddisk might encounter a failure, the user might do something very silly, like deleting all the folders on a harddrive. The result of such errorous behaviour often is severe loss of data.

The solution to that problem is widely known but as widely ignored: backups. Make backups. Most users remember that recommendation for the first time when they suffer from severe loss of data.

The Solution: Time Machine. Mac OS has a very good backup system installed right from the start. The only thing you have to do is attach a backup drive, like a external USB-harddisk to your Mac and point Time Machine to that drive as the main backup drive. Ready.

Fully Automated Full Backup: Time Machine will copy the whole system to the backup drive. But even better: it continuously updates this state by doing so called increment backups, what basically means: only files that changed get copied. It does this every one or two hours or so.

Most important in this system is, that it runs completely without user interaction. You do not need to start the backup or fiddle with configuration. You don't need to do absolutely nothing at all. There ist just one big button in system settings that says: 'Run Time Machine' and you can switch it 'on' or 'off'.

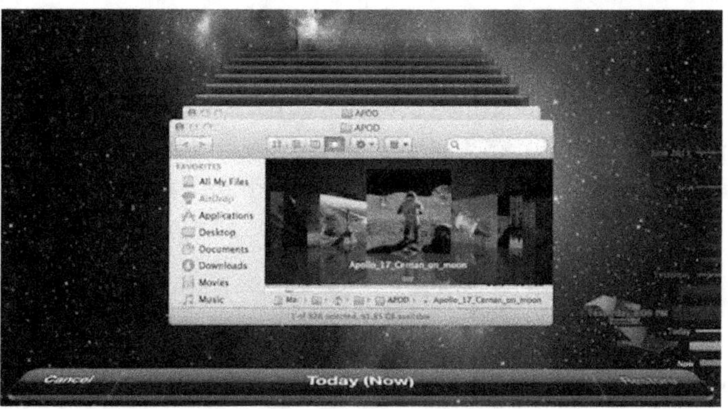

Figure 9.1: Desktop in Time Machine Mode

And that is one of the major features of Time Machine. It does not rely on the user to do anything. That way you cannot make any mistakes. It saves your files seamless and without you even noticing. It runs in the background and never slows down the system. You just don't sense anything besides the secure feeling that your files are save at any time.

That way you always have a full copy of your system harddisk. And with that it gets even better: if your computer has a disk failure (what is quite seldom the case) or you want to move your system from your older Mac to your new purchased Mac (what occurs much more frequent), you just plug that backup drive to your new Mac and the system will copy itself completely over to the new hardware.

System Continuity independend from the Hardware you Use:

After an hour or so (depending on how fast your USB backup drive is) you can just continue working on your new Mac as if nothing had changed at all (besides the new Mac being much faster than the old one of course). Everything is there. Your files, your system configuration, all apps, everything.

Backup to Local Drive or over the Net: Since Mountain Lion you even might choose a network attached drive with a Time Machine compatible server on it as a backup drive. This could of course be a Apple Time Capsule if you want to spend a lot of money for not so much storage space, or any other NAS, even Linux based, like a Synology or QNAP product which all feature Time Capsule compatible servers. With two clicks you have the backup server set up and it runs seamlessly.

Time Machine that way is far more than just a backup system. It is managing your installation independently from the hardware you use.

You may even in case of an emergency boot from that backup drive, as it is a complete and valid installation of your Mac system.

Time Machine was actually together with (the mere eye candy) Cover Flow and Spotlight one of three main features for I wanted a Mac. I really wanted and needed a consistent and seamless backup system, a desktop search that actually worked – and something as cool as cover flow just for kicks. But I got so much more...

9.2   Spaces

Spaces: Virtual Desktops

Again another feature you usually have to install third party software and often even have to pay for it is virtual desktops, in Mac OS called Spaces.

You of course can use this feature excessively. I for my part however only use two virtual desktops. One for my 'office' apps like Email, iMessage, Calender and Contacts, they are allowed to live there on the second virtual desktop, while I work with all the other apps from Eclipse to Pages on the other 'main' desktop.

If you use more than two sometimes orientation becomes a bit hard, but you cannot go wrong with two, as there is always only one 'other' desktop you can switch to.

However this feature does indeed extend your working space and thus improve overview. And as it is built in into the system and is made with the 'usual' Apple quality – meaning it never ever does something wrong, it just works – it is really a helper.

Chapter 10

10.6 Snow Leopard (2009)

10.1   Preview

Preview: Preview files without leaving Finder

You may zoom any file you want in Finder and you see a preview.

The Problem: when you flip through your files in Finder looking for a specific file, you often encounter files with filenames that make it possible, however not sure that it is the file you are looking for. What do you do? Click on it and open it in Pages or Numbers... or continue looking...?

I admit this used to be a more crucial question in former times than today. Because until the arrival of SSDs this process could take up to 10 seconds until the <boop> no, that's not it... wrong file shows up and you close it again. But today loading even a large file into an app takes up nearly no time at all. But still... loading it, scanning through it is much easier with...

Figure 10.1: Finder in Cover Flow with Preview

The Solution: Preview. Preview shows you a... preview of the file clicking the space bar. And the preview is quick. You cannot only see the first page, you can click through all the pages searching for the information you are looking for.

This is much quicker than opening it in the real app, because there is no possibility to edit the file. You just read it. But it helps a lot. That way, files are already showing their content in Finder within the Cover Flow view and pressing the space bar it gets zoomed and you can flip through their pages utilizing the whole screen. This works of course for Pages, Numbers and Keynote files, but of course also for pdfs, every image or audio format you can think of, a lot of video formats, and a lot of other file types, because the Live Preview function is expandable.

10.2   Quicktime X

Quicktime: A Movie Player (and Recorder)

Don't mistake Quicktime for just being a movie player. Of course it is a movie player. But it is also a screen recording tool, a recorder for the built in camera (built in in every Apple Display) and an audio recorder as well – it even has basic video editing functions.

The Problem: This is of course not a problem everybody has. But a computer is a very multi purpose tool and so there might be an overwhelming majority of features not everybody uses.

On other systems, you need third party software that often is not for free, or not very good, often even both, when it comes to record in a video of what's going on on your screen. Not so on the Mac.

Why you should do this in the first place? Well, people want to make a video tutorial or a demonstration of some software they have written or any other purpose you want your actions on the screen recorded for. In-game recordings are quite en vogue these days on the internet and one Youtube: people playing computer games and recording it, put together with explanations, clever remarks or just silly, funny comments or all of that. Some people on Youtube even click around on the internet and comment images and information that can be found there – either to criticize, to clarify or just to have fun.

The Solution: is simple. Use a screen recording software. And as simple as it sounds, most computers don't have a good one handy.

Not so the Mac. Apple just ships a rather good one as part of Mac OS. And they tell everybody so intensely, that most of the users probably have no clue that they have that functionality actually built in into Quicktime right in front of their noses.

And if you want to cut your screen recording, you can of course use iMovie, that also comes with the system for free. But that is just another story...

Life can be so simple.

Chapter 11

10.7 Lion (2011)

Ten years after the first Mac OS-X version finally comes the king: Lion.

Lion was the last Mac OS Steve Jobs presented himself, because only weeks after this last keynote he sadly passed away.

It was the last version he had massive influence in its design. After the Mac had been his baby 25 years ago. And one thing is quite obvious: he wanted to make one last big hit and packed everything in this release that he and his team could dream of.

That resulted in a system that was at first not as stable as usually — what of course was fixed with the first and second update patch. But if you see the sheer list of features that were added to the system and the complexity of the features added (e.g. the integration of iCloud into the whole system, the system apps, like Mail, Calender, etc. but also into the large applications like Pages, Numbers and Keynote, as well as in the big multimedia apps like iPhoto) you might be a bit forgiving that there were still some minor bugs in it in it's first incarnation.

11.1 iCloud

iCloud: Saving everything in the Cloud

This is a big one.

Of course you are used to store things you want to use elsewhere on another computer, in the cloud, like e.g. Dropbox or a similar service. But this is nothing compared to what iCloud offers you! Because iCloud is far from only storing some files on some harddisk in the sky – meaning: *somewhere.*

Let's look at some use cases: when you're on the road, you probably only have your iPhone in your pocket. If you're in a meeting, you have your Macbook. If you're at home on your sofa, you have your iPad in your hands. And if you're in your office, or in your home-office you sit in front of your iMac.

All these devices have a different purpose and use case – that's why they all make sense and have a right to exist.

The Problem: But the problem is, you might want to work with the same data on all of these devices. And you don't want to be bothered with the task of having all your files manually synced over to them. You just want your Pages and Numbers Documents on your iPhone to quickly look something up or write an idea down. You want to find your notes you took on your iPad last night today in your Notes app on your iMac to work with them – seamlessly. You want the music or your new audiobook, you purchased on your Mac available on your iPhone on a walk in the evening. You want your photos taken with your iPhone – and that is: without any interaction on your part. Your iMac should simply store these photos in Fotos. And so on. Often the device you aquire something is not the device you store it or edit it on.

It's the same with Contacts, Calender entries, Reminders, Keynote Presentations, Xcode stuff you write, even your keyboard snippets – yes the Mac can also do that without using third party software. So who does all this sync stuff? You? Probably not.

Figure 11.1: iCloud Web Frontend

The Solution: iCloud syncs absolutely everything (everything that makes any sense, of course). It does all that without you even noticing.

But it does even more: it does not only sync all my devices, it selectively syncs with all devices of my wife and anyone else I want to. So my wife immediately sees when I enter a new calender entry (in a calender I share with her). She has access to my Contacts and I can share with her any Reminders list I want to. This makes cooperation in the family or with colleagues so much easier!

And in the latest incarnation of these iCloud services, the sync has become much more intelligent. It now recognizes when you have not enough free space on your device and the system cleans up the device for you to make room for the new music album or whatever is your latest purchase might be. The other files are not lost, they are still stored in iCloud (and on all of your devices that still have enough storage space free) and you just load them again, when you need them.

So now the old canonical problem that your iPhone has always not enough space free for your newest photos and hd-videos is history. It is indeed history so much, that from now on, you iPhone has *always* enough free space, no matter how many photos you take, because all that this is managed for you in the background without you even noticing.

And of course: if you don't like the idea that some software decides for you which files on you computer to delete, you can completely deactivate these functions. I for myself have these deactivated on my main iMac, because this thing has over 3 TB of space and some large drives attached to it. But my Macbook only has a 256 GB SSD and here this function comes quite handy, so it is activated. The same with iPhone and my iPads. It's up to you to use it or not.

11.2   App Store

Mac App Store: Online Software Store for the Mac

The Problem: are actually three problems. One, getting software onto your computer, two getting it installed and three getting it updated regularly. Of course nowadays there is the infamous internet, that has absolutely everything at hand, esp. also software.

However, it's not so easy. Most software isn't available for free. And in order for you to pay for their product programmers and software companies do nearly everything to make purchasing software online a bit of a headache. And when you bought the software they want to make sure that you don't give it to your brother, your neighbor and who else might be interested in it. So they give you lengthy code-numbers to type in, that are back-checked over the internet with their servers and so on. This is all nothing like elegant or easy.

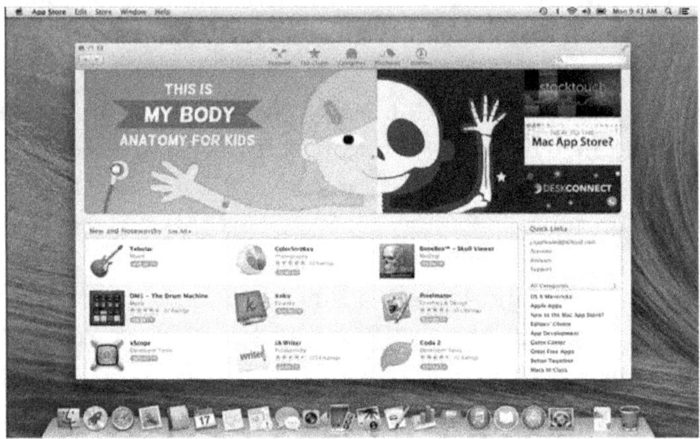

Figure 11.2: The Mac App Store

The Solution: is a consistent software management tool like the App Store. It does all automatically for you. Manages payment, download, installation, copyright issues, everything. The App Store offers you any software you can think of, some of it free, some with some payment mode. But you can access everything with just one click.

By the way: the App Store is not the only software management tool you can install on your Mac. If you e.g. really like Open Source software or Terminal tools, you may also install something like the Homebrew manager that does basically the same with typical Linux style software for your Mac. And the LaTeX distribution for the Mac (with which this book is written), comes with its own updates management tool. And although this is quite handy, you more often than not would wich, all that update stuff might be done by the App Store.

This is the third advantage of the App Store: it does all the updates for you – automatically. In some spare time, when e.g. Power Nap is active (a feature that does a lot of system stuff when your Mac should be in sleep mode) App Store just downloads and installs all the updates for your apps for you. Again: without you even noticing.

So you see, a App Store is not the end of the world. Even Linux has one called "apt-get", but it is of course terminal and text based, but does basically the same thing.

And another thing here is of great importance: with the App Store, Apple generally reduced prices for software dramatically.

The calculation is: if I sell software for $29 or $99 I perhaps sell some 1000 pcs (per year, per day, whatever). If I sell the same thing for $2.99 or $9.99 I of course need to sell 10 times that many, that's 10.000 pcs. But with the App Store with its Millions of users I probably sell even 10 or 100 times more, like 100.000 or even Millions. With that idea, Apple revolutionized the software market. Apps got really cheap for the user and the programmers make a lot more revenue (the latter at least in theory).

Another service, a system like the App Store is capable to offer is that you can easily install the same software, even payed software, on all your computers with just one click, because the App Store, synced over iCloud, already knows when you open it, which apps you have bought and installed on your other computers. So if you purchase some app once, you are allowed to copy it to all your Macs, like any other real world thing. *You* buy something, not your computer.

That also means, the apps you purchase and pay money for are bound to you and your iCloud account, not, like often in the Windows world to your computer hardware. In the Windows world, when you change your hardware (what you often need to, because the newest Windows will demand it), this also means that you encounter problems getting some of your purchased software to work again on the new hardware. On the Mac if you change your hardware, your iCloud account stays and so do all of your purchases.

The topmost fear people who complain when it comes to the

Apple ecosystem, is that it said to be a secluded neighborhood with no possibility to get in or out. This fear not only applies to iTunes but also to the App Store. So: can I then only use Software that is acknowledged by Apple and available in the App Store? Do I have to relinquish open source software and all other non-App Store accredited Apps?

The answer is a clear *no*, of course not! As stated above most of the Apple typical features of Mac OS are just a proposal, an option. You do not have to use it, you do not even have to follow its idea around. You do not have to use the App Store, you do not have to use iCloud, Time Machine or Spotlight. And if you want to install third party apps from the Open Source market, just do so. No problem with that at all.

11.3   Launchpad

Launchpad: Full Screen App Starter

The Problem: You have a lot of apps installed on your system. And when you want to start one, you do not want to search for it or have to remember its name to start it from Spotlight. You just want to start the <beep> thing for god's sake.

On other systems, like Windows, or similar desktops, folks invented a 'start' button to click on which opens a tiny window where all your applications are crammed in. Why? Why not just use your luxuriously large screen to fill with app icons to choose from?

Figure 11.3: Desktop in Launchpad Mode

The Solution: Launchpad. Obviously inspired by iOS, Apple made their app starter full screen. And that is just the right thing. There is so much space on the screen, why not use it to select the app you like.

And like on iOS you can organize the apps in folders, move them around and so on.

I personally like to start the Launchpad with a multitouch swipe on the trackpad – and select the app I want. Very fast, very easy, very intuitive.

11.4 Notes App

Notes App: Take Notes

Ok, a Notes app isn't exactly what you would call exotic, game-changer-killer-app. Isn't Notepad really one of the oldest, simplest and least impressive piece of software you can think of? Programmers first finger exercises?

However, turns out the Notes app is one of my most daily, regularly used apps of them all. And why is this?

The Problem: There are many many thoughts floating around my brain. And experience of my life says: 80-90% of them are gone a few minutes to some hours later. I know this, since I write them down. So if a really interesting, important or in some other way note-worthy idea comes around, I tend to note it down.

And of course you can use whatever paper and pen you have around to do so and put them all these scribbled paper pieces in a shoe-box – if you have a secretary that sorts them afterwords. Well, but I haven't such a secretary.

So where to put all your genius ideas? Of course you can write them each in single text file, what takes up so much time to manage, that you usually already forgot half of your idea, before you even opened the file. Or you put your ideas all in one big Pages file, you call 'Notes'. No problem with that. But to be honest: wouldn't it be nice if you had the means to categorize all your notes, if you could sort them, if they would sync over iCloud with a counterpart Notes app on your other devices? Notes should be available when that one big idea comes about. Immediately. Not so good if you first have to find that Pages file that you called how... 'Ideas'... no... 'Projects'... no... you get my point.

The Solution: If of course a Notes app that does all that and more. The latest incarnation of Apples quite basic notes app has the possibility to do lists with checkable list points for todo lists, it can past almost every format (also HTML snippets), of course hyperlinks, you can import images in every note and comment on them (basically *draw* in them, you can structure your texts and much more. It is a small word processor but not with the focus on writing texts, but taking and managing small snippets... you may call these 'notes'.

The thing about the Notes app and many other similar apps that help you through the day is that they are available on *all* your devices. In a restaurant you may only have your iPhone available to write something down, at home in your living room you have your iPad in your hand while the nobel-price winning idea strikes you. Sometimes you are on the road and have only your Macbook available to write something down. And of course in front of your iMac you have a computer to work with that also has the same Notes app with the same file base. And you won't have to think about syncing your notes from one device to the Mac back and forth, it all has to be done automatically without you even noticing, your notes just have to be there, and they are. It's as simple and as powerful as that.

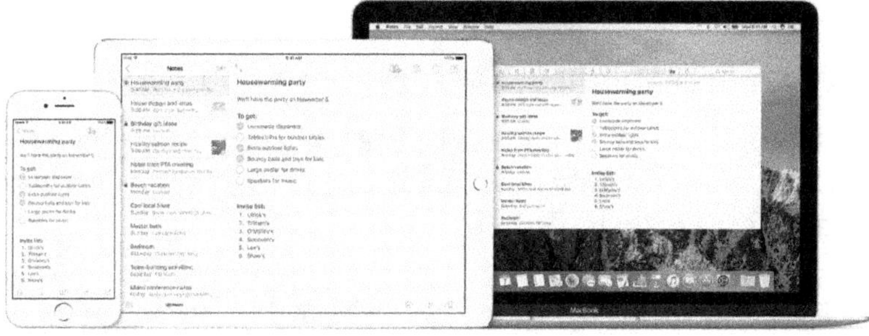

Figure 11.4: Notes App on all devices in sync

Of course the Notes App is something like the prototype of an app that is available on all devices. It basically would make no sense, if you only had it on the Mac but not on iOS (or even worse the other way around). Those apps especially live from their permanent availability.

And of course there are other Notes apps out there on the secondary market, but why should I bother? Of course one or the other might have some handy, cool or even revolutionary feature, but I really don't miss anything with Notes. It does what it is supposed to. It is always in sync with all my other devices so I can switch back and forth between them as I need to and still have the same notes available to work with. Even this book you read at the moment is written in Notes, before typeset in LaTeX.

You probably already found out that I am a fan of software that comes with the system as part of the system (I really dislike software that is shipped with a new computer that has no value at all, fortunately Apple *never* does this).

There are some good reasons to look into the apps that come with the system: this software usually works flawlessly (at least in the Apple part of the World), it uses the latest technology the system has to offer and if the system changes the apps that come with it almost always change with it, you never have to worry that your app still runs with the next system version.

11.5   Autosave & Versions

Autosave & Versions: Saving, Safer than Ever

Some features aren't a big deal. But they are there, when you need them. And one of those small but really helpful features is Autosave and Versions.

The Problem: Every time you close a document you worked with, you get asked the same dumb old question: 'Do you want to save?' and usually the answer is 'yes'. Of course yes! This was the purpose of me working on the file, to keep, what I accomplished, right?

So you have to click the 'yes' or 'ok' button to do that, although it is obvious that this was your intention in the first place. And before you even leave the document, you click that 'Save' command several times (and it is annoying, despite you can to it so fast with the command-s keys). You do that basically every time you think about saving your work. That might be, if you are frantically in fear of loosing just one word or one sentence several times a minute. But then there are those enlightened days when your work flows so tranquilly that you forget about saving completely... and that is that day, when unexpectedly the power supply fails.

The Solution: So what you basically need, to ease your day, to let your focus be on your work and not on saving your work (or forgetting about it altogether), is someone who takes care of that simple but crucial thing: keep up safety automatically. And that does Autosave.

Now you say: but I do not always want to save my changes. Sometimes I want to get back to an older version. Well, you of course still can do that in two ways: first, of course, Undo is still working. Autosave works completely without you noticing and that means, it does not built up any new barriers in front of you that prevent you from working, it just adds more ease!

But what about some earlier changes, aren't they lost with Autosave, because it keeps saving the latest version over the older ones? Well, no. Because of Versions...

Versions is basically a spinoff from Autosave. The idea was, if we already save the users work constantly – and by constantly, I basically mean every keystroke, every little change you do to your work immediately – then we can keep older versions around, or at least their fingerprint to save storage space, and make these also available to the user. It is basically a version system similar to the 'git' tool for programmers.

The Problem: Today data loss is prevented by backups. The only way you still can destroy your work is by deleting it, e.g. you accidentally delete some text passages, in your text file and then save the file. That way you still can kill what you have done, basically because the system cannot distinguish between you deleting text on purpose or deleting text by accident before you save.

The Solution: The only way around that is keep older versions of your files around. So if you find that you deleted text, a whole

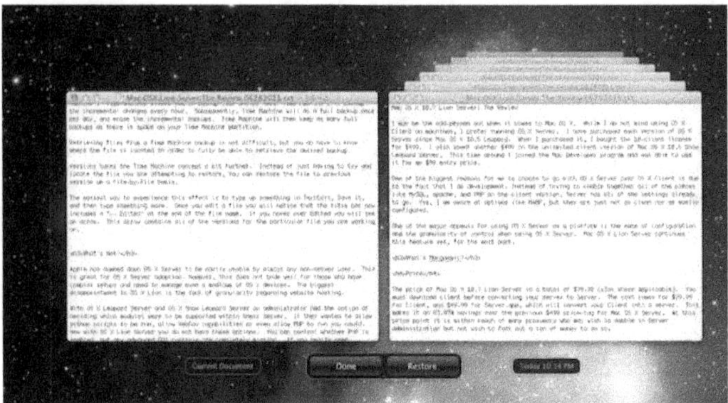

Figure 11.5: Desktop in Versions Mode

chapter or anything similar – of course Versions does not only work with text but with all other kinds of data, like spreadsheets in Numbers, presentations in Keynote and all other apps and their data (if they implement the function that is) – you can just enter the Versions mode, that basically shows you all the past versions of your file compared to the most recent one, and you can select the whole version to make it the most recent one *or*, even better, copy and past lost paragraphs over, because they are still there.

By the way: Autosave also minimizes another old problem that let you save your work frantically every minute or so in former times (and on former operating systems): no data loss any more by crashing applications. It doesn't have to be the Big One. Not only crashing operating systems, bluescreens, kernal panics and similar occations are a hazard to your work but much more obvious reasons: even apps tend to crash sometimes. And of course this is the moment they take your most recent changes with them.

Not any more with Autosave. Because every little change you made is saved like crazy, if a Mac app crashes (what is quite seldom the case as I can assure you), you just start the app again and your work is still there to the last character you entered.

It is so that reliably, that a crash of an app in the middle of my work not even gives me the slightest jolt, because I *know*:

everything's all right, everything's save, everything's saved.

So Versions is basically another mechanism in Mac OS that helps you not loose any of your work. This is another big relieve that helps you a lot to focus on your work and not on what your tool demands.

11.6   Multi Touch

Multi Touch: Use more than one Finger on your Desktop

Sounds a bit crazy. You usually manipulate a computer with a mouse pointer on the screen that rather precisely resembles the movements of a mouse in your hand on the screen. This thing usually has one or more click controls (mouse buttons) – and that's it already, what you got to control your graphical user interface.

The Problem: This is state of the art since Xerox invented the graphical user interface in the 1970s – and Steve ripped them off and created the Mac with their idea. Funnily Bill Gates then ripped Steve off and created Windows with their idea. And since then everybody tried to rip Microsoft off, but they somehow managed to stay on top of the graphical user interface business.

A lot of improvements happened since then to the graphical user interface – but the mouse is still more or less the same. Ok, it became digital, it became optical, some got really a lot of buttons... but you still move it around with your hand and click from time to time, right?

And now, almost unnoticed, Apple adds another input method to the desktop: Multi Touch.

The Solution: Multi Touch was the crystallization point from wich on the development of the iPhone started in the early 2000. An Apple engineer showed Steve a new display technology that was able to detect more than one finger at a time, meaning, e.g. two fingers at a time or, three – you get the idea. Multi Touch was born and with it the real revolutionary genius handling of iPhone and iPad.

Multi Touch allows much more than point and click. An nearly unlimited amount of gestures can be used to control the desktop. One finger moves the mouse pointer, two fingers bring up a context menu, three fingers hold and move windows or files around. Four fingers sliding down for Expose view, four finger spreading out for Desktop view with all windows out of the way and four fingers moving towards each other to get to Launchpad. And a lot more, including fingers moving over the edge of the trackpad, rotating, etc. etc.

At first glance this if of course highly irritating but when you get used to it it becomes highly elegant.

Chapter 12

10.8 Mountain Lion (2012)

12.1　Fusion Drive

Fusion Drive: Fast and Large Mass Storage

If you ask me: this exactly is genius.

The Problem:　Today you have two types of mass storage technologies on the market: harddisks and SSDs. Basically harddisks offer masses of space, like Terabytes (=trillions of bytes) but they are slow, as they have a lot of mechanical parts. SSDs on other hand are new, expensive and for that reason small, like some 100 Gigabytes (=billions of bytes), but they are blazingly fast.

In those times of real Multimedia, where you have fotos, music and videos stored on your computer, you acutally easily fill even terabytes. So obviously today you need a lot of space. But this mass storage space should at the same time be fast, contemporarily fast, meaning, available to the user without any noticeable delay. But the technologies you have for that is harddisks = large and slow, or SSDs = small and fast. How can you have a mass storage in your computer that does the magic trick: large and fast.

The Solution:　Well, you guessed it, Fusion Drive does this trick. The basic idea is that you don't use all of your 2 or 3 Terabytes of files on your computer all day.

How does Fusion drive do the trick? A Fusion Drive, the name suggests it already, is two drives combined – 'fusion' of both worlds. A slow and large harddisk combined with a small but fast SSD. And then you take each advantage and compensate each weakness.

OS-X just keeps track of what the user needs: files that are requested often are stored on the SSD, others that are requested near to never are stored on the slower harddisk. That way, most of the time you request files from the SSD and get them with full SSD speed. On the other hand you can store up to 3 Terabytes of data on you Fusion Drive. Seamlessly.

And of course all of your system files are stored on the SSD from where they load really fast.

The management, which files are stored on the SSD and which ones are stored on the harddisk is invisibly done by the system. And the system does this of course dynamically. When a file gets requested more often, it is physically moved to the SSD. If you don't use a file for days and weeks, it is physically moved to the harddisk. The user has no clue if the file he uses came from the SSD or from the harddisk.

12.2   Power Nap

Power Nap: Do Standard Tasks while you're Asleep

The Problem: Loading email, updating apps, backing up, syncing files. What do these tasks have in common? They suck.

As a user you don't want to be bothered with these. Email just should be there, when you want to read it. Apps should just be up to date. Always. Without you noticing. And backups should have all your necessary files stored securely, but please not with you interacting with it or being held up by it, slowing down the computer or making files not accessible or something like that.

All these tasks, the computer should not only do in the background, but when nobody is using it. That way it has full power, full network bandwidth, full disk access to do these things quick and without bothering anyone.

So Apple invented Power Nap.

The Solution: Power Nap just does these tasks and many more, when the computer is in power save mode, hence the name. It's working in its sleep. It's awake while sleeping...

During power save, without waking up e.g. the display, the computer just syncs all your data, like contacts, notes, reminders, fotos, Spotlight indexing etc.

So when you wake the computer up to continue working, guess what? All these background tasks are done, your email is there, everything is updated, while you (or at least the Mac) slept.

12.3   Dictation

Dictation: The Mac Writes what you Say

This is way longer in the Mac than Siri and much longer than most people would know.

But in this latest incarnation the Mac OS Speech-to-Text engine became really usable, as now, the system loads all the data it needs to understand your voice onto your Mac and uses it locally what dramatically speeds up the speech recognition and the response time.

The Problem: If you have experience with dictating, it is of course much faster than typing. And this is a natural speech engine, what basically means that you can talk as usual, instead of speaking. just. one. word. at. a. time... like it was necessary in former times with less elaborate systems.

The Solution: Load the Speech-to-Text files from Apple (basically a mouseclick in the system settings) and you can dictate any text, any email, anything you want instead of typing it.

This is not Siri. You cannot tell the Mac to search a file or open an app or something similar. But you can very comfortably dictate text.

12.4   Text-to-Speech

Text-to-Speech: Why Read Things Yourself.

This is a rather old feature of the Mac. But it is very handy.

In 1984, Steve Jobs didn't introduce the Mac – the Mac introduced himself. Using the forefather of all text-to-speech engines. This did not quite sound like a human at all but it was a funny gimmick that others, like Commodore with their Amiga were eager to copy. (Anyway, if you look at Commodore and Apple, you find that the C64 was kind of a rip off of the Apple II and the Amiga was nothing more than a rip off of the Mac...)

The Problem: Of course you can read any text you come around. But in a lot of situations it is more comfortable to listen to the text, while... having your eyes closed an concentrate on the content... doing something else, like working... excerpt what you are hearing... whatever you want having your eyes free for it.

The Solution: Today's text-to-speed engines are nothing like the computer voice of 1984's Mac any more. They sound 97% like a natural voice and you – if you are a little tolerant – are able to listen to a longer text without loosing concentration or consciousness. This is quite kind of a new way of reading. You don't read yourself. You let it read to you.

Chapter 13

10.9 Maverics (2013)

No more cats available. So, for codenames, Apple switches from big cats to Californian landmarks.

13.1 Finder Tags

Finder Tags: Keywords to find your files quicker

The Problem: Folders are rather restricted ways of sorting files. The metaphor of a folder or directory comes from real drawers or folders in real life. In real life you have a real piece of paper and you need to put it somewhere. So you pack papers that in some sense deal with the same issue together in one folder, e.g. the plans for a house together with the invoice of the architect and the contact information of the real estate agent.

But then these papers are in that place, just like the papers in reality and you can only find them and retrieve their information if you look into exactly that folder. The files on the computer basically are restricted like in reality, if you treat them like real-world pages of paper und real world folders. If you forget where you put the folder or forget that you also put the real estate agent's phone number into that folder, you're basically fu... – well, you won't find it.

In the beginning computers used that metaphor widely. A file was perceived as some (digital) piece of paper and put in a folder. There it lived happily ever after until you found it there, used it, edited it, printed it, you get the idea.

But computers are capable of much more virtuality than the real world. Computers are capable of doing so much more than that. A computer e.g. is able to automatically make an index of all the files and their contents in all folders to find these files quick and easily, in case you don't remember where you put them – what is very likely as some files might belong into more than one folder!

This is an important recognition, why I repeat it here to let the idea sink in: 'some files might belong into more than one folder!'

Let's say you have a folder for your new house but also one for your new piece of land, where you want to built your house on. The contact information of your architect might belong into both folders. And other than with real paper you of course just may make a copy of the contact info and put one copy info both folders.

Problem is: you now have the information two times and if you want to change something or add his new web address you have to change both files (and have to remember that there are two files with one kind of information in the first place!).

So what are you gonna do? You of course can set a symbolic link on the file in the other folder. That way you can access one file from two places. Not bad.

But still one file is the 'real' one and the other 'file' is just a link to it. Additionally this whole arrangement of files placed in folders is very ineffective when you look for files. Of course you can use Spotlight. But isn't there a better, more flexible, easier to search way?

Well, there is. It is called Finder Tags.

The Solution: Tags are treated badly, although they are a very elegant solution. Tags are kind of a replacement to folders, but nobody seems to know or care. Not even the guys at Apple.

They all seem to perceive Tags as a collection of keywords that help search. But this again is old school thinking. Tags are nothing less than the solution to the one-file-one-folder problem. Because you can think of Tags as folder, but you can place any file in as many 'folder' = Tags, as you like. If you search for a file via Spotlight, the Tags obviously will help you find it. But if you want to, you can use the Tags as a flexible 'folder' hierarchy that leads you to your files very quickly. And what else is a filesystem for than to find your files and work with them. Nobody gets a nobel-price for the most beautiful directory structure.

Additionally you can work with Tags very flexible: You not only need to give files tags that stay forever, like hewn in stone. You may also use tags like 'important', 'new' or 'later' to show their temporary status and remove or change them later when the status has changed. That way, if you look for all files that are 'important' in Spotlight, all the files tagged 'important' show up.

Chapter 14

10.10 Yosemite (2014)

14.1   Maildrop

Maildrop: Email with (really) Large Attachments

The Problem: Email attachments usually are limited to 10 or even 8 MB, depending on the configuration of the mailservers they have to pass on their way to their destination.

And in times of nearly unlimited use of fotos, audio and video this limit is increasingly archaic. Even smaller pdf files with some fotos in them or average presentation slides easily swell to more than double or threefold that without any struggle.

The Solution: So what's this and how can they even do this, they probably can't change settings on mailservers, don't they? Of course the Mac team came up with solution...

With Maildrop this limit is obsolete. It indeed is replaced by a new limit Apple sets to email attachments: 5 GB. How they do it? Quite simple: if an email is sent with an attachment larger than the usual limit, the system uses the internet mail service to send the email and separates the attachment from it. The attachment is loaded to an Apple server.

Then when the email is received by the destination user, two things can happen: if he also has a Mac, email and attachment are reunited in his mail app, without him even noticing. He just receives an email with a large attachment. If he as another computer, the email he receives contains a link to the attachment to download from the Apple server.

Again this solution is as transparent and as seamless for the user as possible. But the most important thing is: it breakes an old and seemingly fixed rule of the internet: that email attachments are limited to 8 MB.

14.2 iPhone Calls

iPhone Calls: Using your Mac as a Headset

How often do you sit in front of your computer, you hear your mobile phone ring, but you don't know exactly where it is, because it hides somewhere in your jacket, your briefcase, in your entrance hall, whereever.

The Problem: Every mobile phone has a big problem: it's mobile. So, unless you are a full blown control freak, that basically means it is never where you expect it to be, because by definition it has no fixed place where you may expect it in the first place.

This decisively collides with the fact that an increasing number of phone call are done using the mobile phone.

The Solution: To make this situation more comfortable, you can now use all of your Apple devices, that is of course all Macs but also all iOS devices you have around, to answer your iPhone calls. And even better, of course you also can start a call from all of these devices! This finally makes your Mac a telephone!

That by the way has nothing to do with the facetime network. These are phone calls that use your real cell phone number and your provider's cell phone network. You of course may also use facetime, if you want to.

Chapter 15

10.11 El Capitan (2015)

This is of course a large mountain in Yosemite. And it is a Toc release, what means, not so many new features but refinements like increasing speed and efficiency.

15.1   iCloud Drive

iCloud Drive: Store all your files in the Cloud – seamlessly

It is kind of a natural evolution of computing and saving data.

The Problem: In former times you had a computer and on that were all your apps (that back then were called 'programs') and of course all your files. Then computers began to be everywhere, but that did not help a lot as still your files and apps were on just *one* of these computers – often not the one available at the place you just were as these things were damn local too. So all the other computers standing around everywhere, at other offices, your friends house, in an internet cafe were basically dead meat. Because your files were not there.

To help out at least in your company where you worked, soon files went on a server in the basement. So every time you logged on at any computer within the company network, you were at least able to access your files from there.

But then came the smartphones. And the Tablets. And of course the laptops. And again, the server in the basement of your company – or your home – wasn't of so much use at all, even if it had all your files. As this server wasn't available everywhere, as it wasn't on the internet. And VPNs (Virtual Private Networks), simulated, encrypted networks over the internet weren't just a brillant solution, as they were hard to configure.

So servers on the internet came along. Like Dropbox. You now could place your files there (if you trusted them and their encryption standards) and access them from your iPhone or any other mobile device. The idea is: it doesn't matter which device you use, your files are always already there you give it a try.

The Solution: And then Apple came late to the party, as usual and did all the things right that others (partially) got wrong and that way the managed to, as usual, be able to make everything better.

So while iCloud alone makes files available to all your computer over the internet, iCloud drive opens that mechanism to literally every file you want to have in your cloud space. It's not only 'only' files from your Apple Apps that store their files in the cloud, now, you just get to finder and place any file you like on iCloud Drive, like you would with Dropbox or any other service.

Of course iCloud Drive is just a built in Dropbox in Mac OS. But as it is built in, you can do a lot things better than with any addon. E.g. finds Spotlight 'of course' every file on iCloud Drive as if it were stored locally on your harddisk. Of course does Mac OS copy all your files to iCloud Drive automatically and sync any change you do at once to the Cloud, completely without you noticing, perfect transparency. And of course is iCloud drive as well a app specific place for the files you create with pages or numbers as well as a general purpose online cloud drive for any other file you create.

That way it is also a great offsite backup system, as your file automatically get copied to a offsite server, so if your flat burns down to the ground and even your server in the basement gets grilled, your files are still there on Apple's servers. And as all files are synced over all your computers you automatically have a copy of your all files on your Macbook and on your old spare Mac as well.

Oh, and there's *just one more thing*: Apple does really everything to make your data as save as humanly possible – despite them being on a cloud server and thus potentially accessible to everyone on the internet. Of course the files are encrypted with top notch encryption methods. Of course Apple themselves have no access to your files – only you have.

But additionally, all the files are *not* stored on Apple servers, what at first sounds counter-intuitive to security. But it isn't. Indeed it improves security again as Apple splits up your files into small chunks that are stored on different servers like from Amazon, Google and other big players with loads of storage.

So if someone breaks into the Apple servers and (unlikely) manages to break or somehow find a way around encryption, he still has only parts of your files that are not of much use. In order to get the rest of the files, he also has to break into servers of Google, Amazon and all the others. And that is very unlikely, because these all use very different systems and usually hackers manage to break into a system using a security issues, basically an error in the server system. To break into so different systems like these other big players use at the same time is highly unlikely. So your files that way are ultimately save.

Chapter 16

10.12 Sierra (2016)

16.1   Siri

Siri: Talk to your Mac

Finally they did it. Since the iPhone 4S everybody was waiting for Siri to come to the Mac.

The Problem: The problem is that there wasn't a problem. Not one that could be fixed with Siri. Perhaps this is why Siri on the Mac is implemented so lukewarm.

Of course you now can tell your Mac what files you want to use next and let Siri find them for you. But who cares? I, for now more than a year, have Siri on the Mac and I must admit: I don't use it at all. Not for finding files, not for starting apps, not for adding calender entries or reminders. I just don't use it at all.

It somehow is so far away from how I traditionally use my Mac with the Keyboard and the Magic Trackpad, that I constantly forget the option to simply talk to it. And despite it's there I don't miss it at all.

Additionally Siri on the Mac does have problems with things I'd expect from 'her'. E.g. I would like to tell her "Shut down the Mac in 10 minutes", but all she responds is that she cannot do this. O...k. Why...? Isn't she the computer in the first place? I can! And I'm just sitting in front of that thing.

And generally we don't get along very good. If I want to dictate something, still the old Speech-to-Text engine comes around and not Siri with her artificial intelligence that 'understands' what you say and thus gets more of your words right.

For me clicking on an icon in Dock starts an app faster than Siri can – and way more reliable.

And finding my files, I still use the old fashioned way with Finder. It isn't slower and usually I know exactly where and what I am looking for.

And if I happen to search something, I use Spotlight. The thing with search terms is that often Siri has a hard time to understand *exactly* the search words I am using. And search just is of no use at all when I say 'last used pages documents' and Siri comes up with a 'least trusted rage' Web search. It is clearly more productive to just type the search terms exactly like you want them into Spotlight.

Basically, I don't know exactly what I ever wanted to ask my Mac. Perhaps that is the problem for me. And from the Star Trek thing, like 'Siri, analyze all my files to give me the highest probability for a best selling new book topic' still is in a Galaxy far far away.

Perhaps there will be a killer application for Siri in Mac OS versions to come...

16.2   Universal Clipboard

Universal Clipboard: Copy&Paste Unlimited

This is another one of those little helpers that you won't use on a daily basis, but if you need it, it's there. It transforms the idea of a clipboard you can copy things to and paste them from to an abstract level, beyond physical computers. It becomes kind of 'cloud' clipboard, but without some cloud running.

The Problem: Our work gets more and more split up between devices. And since the Mac OS and iOS environment is the first combination of operating systems in history that are really equal in the sense that you can seamlessly work with large applications like Pages, Numbers and Keynote on both plattforms with the same files without any conversion, you don't work on your computer *or* have fun on your mobile devices, but you can use all of these devices to do your work – whichever fits your purpose best.

I for myself often take notes on the iPad, because I can think better, when I don't sit in front of my computer. Somehow this less obstrusive little device and the places I can use it (in the garden, in the living room etc.) lets my creativity flow more freely. The same goes with the iPhone. Since Siri understands so darn good, what I tell her, I often use the iPhone as a next generation dictation machine. I tell Siri my ideas, and she writes it down in a note. No transcribing from speech to text anymore.

The Solution:　And that way I also do research and come across things I directly want to use on my Mac. And that is where universal clipboard is handy (at least for me). No fiddling around, how I get this file from the mobile device over to my computer. Just copy it, paste on the Mac and it's there. A little helper in the background, but important, because it bridges a large chasm between the devices, invisible, but there if you need it.

16.3　Optimized Storage

Optimized Storage: files only in the cloud, available on demand, automatic deletes nonsense files

Sometimes you think: why are they doing this now, and not some 10 or 20 years ago? Apple is a strange company. They invented so much that sometimes, they seem to forget the really easy things.

Usually dealing with trash is not one of the most attractive and sexy things at all. But on the computer it's not so bad, as trash there at least doesn't stink, right?

And part of handling trash on a computer is the question of emptying the Trashcan.

And it doesn't seem to be such a hard job to do, right? Even PC Tools from 1990 on an operating system called 'DOS' could do a kind of first-in-first-out thing with its trashcan. It's not so hard at all. If you put something into the trash, what means you already had decided to delete it, it is just a luxury feature to be able to eventually get it back. This simply addresses the really old computer rule that 'delete' is the command you use exactly the day before you really *need* a file. So you obviously want to keep it just for another while, before it is absolutely save to terminate it, because you really won't need it any more.

But that is old school. Today you don't type 'delete', you just drag and drop files into the Trashcan (on your Desktop or in the Dock).

And after some days or weeks or even years, you probably really won't need a file any more.

And to make things not too simple, you could indeed put a bit of 'intelligence' in this function that finally gets rid of all your old and not-wanted-any-more-files:

let it e.g. keep (normally small) documents, like from Pages, Numbers, Keynote or its Microsoft counterparts longer in the trashcan, longer meaning let's say for one year.

You might want to finally terminate (often large) apps earlier, let's say after 1 month or even a week, basically because you probably will be able to get these again from the app-store or some other place on the internet (and probably then an updated and improved version of them).

And then you should terminate really large file like hd-movies quicker, just because they are large and deleting one of them probably weighs more and thus frees more diskspace than deleting 1000 of your own personal Pages files. So this step is quite efficient, right?

But you might want the system do this only, if the file is not made with your own copy of iMovie, meaning, they are probably also not the only copies of this material around. On the other hand if you made them by your own, they probably *are* the only copy available and for that reason should be kept around longer, because they are probably the only specimen of their kind. You get the idea...

But unfortunately the Mac Trashcan was miles from that for a long time.

The Problem: This is really a big one, construction area, middle ages, there was a lot to do here... All of this and more could have been implemented into the Trashcan a long time ago.

But Apple chose to have just one feature at all: let the user select the 'Empty Trashcan' command to get rid of all that old stuff from time to time – and just by himself. Why implement some 'intelligent' stuff at all?

Usually this command 'Empty Trashcan' was used when the free space on your harddisk became magically low and you were even more astonished to learn that this was the case, because the Trashcan (!) meanwhile used up to 678 Gigabytes on your 1 TB Disk.

When you then used the 'Empty Trashcan' command, Trashcan would start to delete everything. Everything was put into the shredder. It terminated apps you seem to remember that you had them for some minutes on you harddisk, before you decided to get rid of them, on that summer evening 3 years ago the same way as it would terminate the Numbers table you moved to the Trashcan yesterday, not knowing that you would need the information stored there – and only there – in another 4 days from now.

And to make things even more ridiculous Trashcan tried to empty *all* the invisible Trashcan directories on *all* your other harddisks at once. So if you needed disk space let's say on your small but fast system disk, but your large media-USB-disk was perfectly fine and you really would have liked it if Trashcan would have kept your deleted music files for some more days, you had been fu****. Because Trashcan just did not think so far.

And to make things worse: Trashcan puts a Trashcan on every file system, no matter what. So if you ever delete a file on a small usb-stick, Trashcan of course wouldn't delete it but keep it in a Trashcan folder. That means, you have a 2 GB stick, you have a 1 GB movie on it, you want to delete the movie to put another 1.4 GB movie on the stick, it won't work. When you try to copy the second file to the stick, *despite the stick is empty in Finder (!)* Finder will tell you that there is not enough space on the stick left. Why? Because there is a hidden system directory on it now that contains the 1 GB movie – and even on user demand won't get rid of it. And even worse: when you select 'Empty Trashcan' Trashcan will begin to empty all Trashcans throughout the whole system. What utter nonsense!

This had been of course not acceptable and is just a miracle how this situation was able to persist for such a long time.

The Solution   Of course not all of that addressed above, is solved. But the new memory management 'Optimized Storage' does some important things right.

If you look for this new functions to configure them you probably will be surprised. They do not reside in the System Preferences (as they should), but in the 'About this Mac' feature and there in Hard-Disks behind a 'Configure' button. Strange.

There you find four topics that should help you to manage your system storage efficiently.

Let's start with the third option (for logical reasons): this option *automatically* terminates files from your Trashcan that are there for more than 30 days. Simple, but ok. This is an ok solution but miles from what I suggested above would be clever. But for the moment: let's be happy that this feature that we already had in the DOS PC Tools in 1990, finally found its way into the most advance operating system of them all in the year 2016 A.D. Don't complain, be happy.

Another feature in some different way addresses the 'large movie' issue, at least partially. Option two deletes movies and TV shows from the iTunes directory if you already have seen them. That is an ok function, that however is very iTunes centered. All the other movies and media files that are on your harddisk are not affected by it – unfortunately. If you don't use iTunes to buy movies and TV shows at all this whole function doesn't help you a bit. Of course that these are deleted from your harddisk doesn't mean they are gone: you of course can load them again if you decide to watch them a second time...

The first feature goes beyond the Trashcan. It basically removes files you never use from your harddrive (mainly Documents and Fotos), keeping just the copy of them on iCloud, and loads them from iCloud in case you need them. That comes handy on let's say a Macbook, where you have very limited disk space. But to be honest, on my main iMac I have that feature disabled because I want *all* of my files on *my* computer. I might be old school.

The last option is called 'Reduce Chaos', what leads me to think: there is no *chaos* on my computer, friends. And the second thing is: I just don't want to have a algorithm decide to delete my stuff. Sorry. I am old school.

So there is a lot going on, but in my book, to optimize the Trashcan a bit more would be more of an improvement than these functions. But as you – as always – can disable them you may just choose the ones that fit you.

Chapter 17

10.13 High Sierra (2017)

High Sierra (you guessed it by the name) is a Toc Version. That means not so many new features but improvements under the hood and on the speed front. So again this Mac OS Version has a lot of refinements and evolutionary improvements, it even has some revolutionary new features, like the APFS File System and Virtual Reality Support, but this all is 'under the hood' and not directly visible to the user.

Chapter 18

What I Still Miss

Functions that Mac OS still not has...

A Mac, contrary to it's image in public, is a rather open system. You can even install Windows on it – but who would want that? I mean, seriously? (The only reason I can think of is to prove how much slower Windows is on the exact same hardware.)

The general tendency is that nowadays computers have a lot more features to offer than anyone is able to or has time to use.

But still some things astonishingly lack. And my personal favourites of these are here. This is my wish-list for future Mac OS versions:

Directory Information Cache

Filesystem should cache the directory information of external disks for quicker access after disk power save

What is my Problem?   Usually the system disk of your Mac is not enough. That doesn't necessarily mean, that it too small, to smallish dimensioned by Apple, that just means that, no matter how large your disk is, some day it will be full and that you these days can do so much with your computer (fotos, videos, music, audiobooks, and all that really storage intensive stuff) that you probably will have some additional storage solutions attached to your Mac.

These might be USB harddisks on your desk and/or even server space in your basement or offsite somewhere.

And all of that works Apple-typically fine. The USB disks are of course not a problem at all, and the network connection to the server also works maximum reliably, no matter what system you use, a Mac server, a Linux server, a Windows server and their typical networking protocols. The Mac speaks every language.

So all is good, right?

Well, no. And here is why: usually these external or even remote disks are only used sporadically. They have always time when they are not accessed at all. And during this periods they will go into energy saving mode, what means, they shut down and stop. The other way around, that means that they just have to restart, when you access them.

And that sucks. You click on your external USB harddisk and what happens? Nothing. The thing spins up, it loads the directory sectors, and then... finally... after seconds of annoying waiting... there it is. This is just seconds, but wasn't the Mac all about responsiveness?

The same thing with network attached storages and other servers. Either the disks have to start before the system responds or, even worse, you cannot reach a file system, just because another task is pushing data to that server full-speed-no-matter-what.

My Solution? Cache the file system information. Not to be misunderstood: don't cache the files, just the directory information. Just cache the directory tree of any external disk or network drive. They don't change so often and so much and even if they do, just set a 'dirty bit' and update the information. That way, if you access the sleeping USB disk, you will get the first directory level while it spins up, you get the second while it reads the directory sectors, when the system finds out that the directory had changed (while the disk slept, for gods sake?) it will tell you, kick you out and you may begin from the start, if everything is in sync (what will be the case 99% of the time) you can work with the disk already, while it wakes up. Would be a major improvement in working with those external drives.

The same applies to network drives. Of course here the danger that the directory structure might not be up-to-date is higher, as probable more that one person accesses the files of the server. But even here, changes might just affect directories you don't even access and you just don't mind, if the cached directories are updated in the background while you browse through just completely different directories or not. In case they are not up-to-date, same thing happens as with the external drive. You will be complimented out back to the root level. Not such a big deal at all.

Use More than One Language

Switch languages for text-to-speech and speed-to-text modules

I completely get it: there is just one and only language on the planet: english. But to be frank and honest: there isn't. And if you happen to grow up and even live in a country where english is not the first, not even the second language, you might realize that there is indeed more than one language on planet earth, they are actively spoken, people actually use them.

I for my case use german and english a lot. Always changing between these two. I write texts and even books in english and german. I read texts on the internet in english (mostly) and german and I want to dictate and listen to texts in english as well as in german.

But there is a problem: If you use your Mac with german language (as I do) you of course can use the text-to-speech engine to let it read german texts aloud. All well so far. But if you have an english text, like a website or something and you want your (german) Mac to read that also, you're stuck. Because it won't. It will sound very peculiar, as when the german speech engine tries to pronounce english word.

You just cannot tell it to read that website with the english text-to-speech engine, because there is basically no menu command for that.

I reduce the problem to the menu entry, because you indeed can download and use english text-to-speed modules also on a german language Mac. You even can use it – on the terminal with the 'say' command and an english voice. But the text has to be available as non-formatted text file only. So quickly read a website is just not possible.

My Solution: And it could be so easy and simple! You just need a menu entry that not only says 'Read this' but 'Read this in German' and another one 'Read this in English'. Just implement that – please! – and you will make a lot of customers in not english-speaking countries so much happier!

The same thing applies for speech-to-text (this is the other way around, basically dictating with your voice into text inside the computer).

The Dictate function works quite well, even if it is not as good as Siri on the iPhone. But it is ok. Unfortunately, you cannot just choose if you want to have a english or german speaking secretary. If your Mac is configured as a german Mac you just can talk to him in German. And that is again a pity as there is no principle obstacle to just choose 'Dictation English' or 'Diktat Deutsch'. The files and functionality is available, no question.

Clever Trashcan

Better Trashcan functions (see Sierra: Optimized Storage)

Clever Clipboard

A more clever clipboard, with functions like, retype last entry, show all I copied today, etc...

The Clipboard is without question the most often used and at the same time most invisible tool of them all. We all press command-c (copy) and command-v (paste) on a daily basis never even thinking about it any more.

But this seams a mistake. The Clipboard could offer some more features that would make work so much easier. Like e.g. a repeat function. Often you enter something into a form, like on a website, you press 'ok' but somehow the website decided to forget everything and start over from null. What you would want is *not* type in all the information again, but have the computer remember what you just already typed some seconds ago. The same applies for filenames you entered and similar situations. Additionally nobody knows why you still need third party software to have some kind of a copy/paste history to get back to. Often you have to copy two or more things again and again and it would be great to be able to paste the last 10 items by e.g. clicking command-1 to command-0 or similar. So it won't be copy, past, copy paste, copy paste, but copy, paste, paste, paste... you get the idea.

Choose Image Format at Saving

When I save a picture from the internet in Safari I want to already choose its file format

There are a lot of different media formats around. And picture formats are not the least many ones. So when I save an image in

Safari I'd find it appropriate to be offered right inside the save-dialog to choose the format I'd save the image in. E.g. it should be possible to save an image that comes as a .png as .jpg. Today I need to save the .png, have to start Preview, select export and save it as .jpg, which is much more time consuming.

These suggestions not only show what small additions I would expect from Mac OS to become perfectly perfect, but also, how far Mac OS still *is* very very good that it comes down to these little quirks that I miss.

Chapter 19

The Author

A Few Words about My Background

In 1984 I started out with my first computer: a Commodore 128D.
I quickly switched to the more modern Commodore Amiga that I
then used from 1985 until 1990. I didn't know at that time that
the Amiga, as well as the competing Atari ST was a Mac rip-off.
As all Commodore Home-Computers obviously were. The famous
C64 had already been an Apple II rip-off.

From 1991 on to 2009 I then used several Windows PCs (most
of them I built myself) with DOS and Windows 3.1 in the beginning
and then cycling through the diverse (and increasingly colorful)
incarnations of Windows: from Windows 3.11 to Windows 95
and Windows 98 over to the more stable Windows NT 4.0, then
Windows 2000, Windows XP. I skipped Windows Vista and went
directly to Windows 7 – but just for a short time.

And all these Windows versions had one thing in common: they
cost me a lot of nerves and time and energy to tame. Windows, at
least on my level of usage, almost never did as expected. Things
went unnecessarily slow, cpu-time was consumed by antivirus
checks, things tended to crash instead of working properly.

From 2008 on I was looking for an alternative. At that time
Linux was more and more recommended on the internet and pro-
moted as a desktop computer OS. I tried (K)Ubuntu Linux in

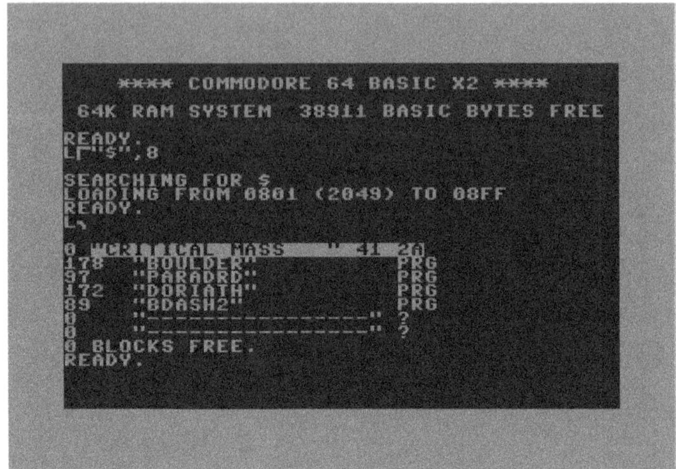

Figure 19.1: Commodore C64/C128 "Desktop"

Figure 19.2: Windows XP Desktop

2009 and 2010. But it also never did what it was supposed to and what was promised. It was a somehow more intelligently designed system than Windows. One could feel the many academic solutions that went into the UNIX system since its first installments in the 1970s. However, as a desktop system it lacked really a lot, so in sum it wasn't better than Windows, the in part crucial problems just were in different places.

Figure 19.3: (K)Ubuntu Desktop

Then – with some delay of about 2 years – I saw the iPhone presentation (»Are you getting it? These are not three separate devices! This is one device. And we call it iPhone«) and my whole (computer-)world changed. I began to let Apple come on my radar. I hesitated. Apple was to me just one thing: expensive. More expensive than I intended to spend. So I tested a Hackintosh installation of Leopard an a 8 year old laptop – and after about 10 seconds and I knew: this system was absolutely brillant. It ran like hell on a laptop that would not even run properly with the Windows XP it came with in the first place.

So in 2011 I finally bought a Macbook Pro with Snow Leopard – despite the seemingly high price. This thing was great. It was reliable, fast, brillant in any way. I then switched to a Mac Mini with a 27" Thunderbolt Display in 2013. And finally, I got an iMac 27" in 2015. These latter computers from Apple are all by far the best computers I ever had the privilege to use. By far.

For input I today use a Apple Bluetooth Keyboard II and a

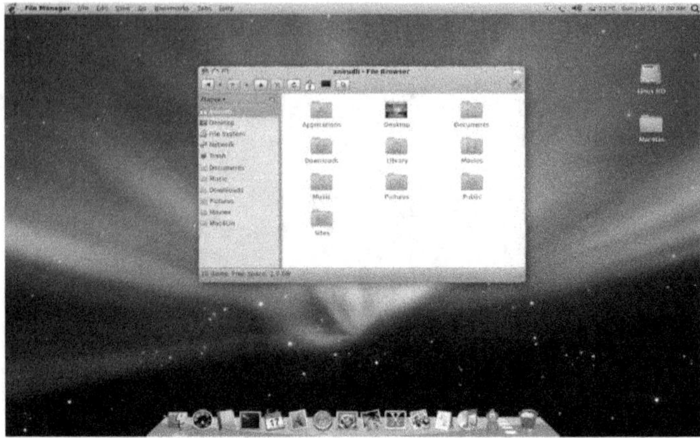

Figure 19.4: Mac 'Snow Leopard' Desktop

Magic Trackpad II. These two serve me perfect. Especially the Magic Trackpad with the built in rechargeable batteries and the large surface area is a beautiful input device. It is much more elegant than having your right hand clinging to a mouse most of the time. It has something of Minority Report, if you know what I mean.

Even if the Apple Magic Mouse is really a great mouse, the Trackpad is much more elegant. And additionally, if you use a Macbook, there is no more inconsistency in the way you move your mouse pointer around the screen any more. Trackpad on the iMac, trackpad on the Macbook. Even the Multi-Touch Displays of iPad and iPhone is similar. It all becomes one usability continuum. Great!

So when I say, I know all these systems, Windows, Windows NT and the followers, even Linux, like Ubuntu and Debian, I even used and administrated a Solaris (the Unix sported by Sun), I don't say too much. Trust me.

Chapter 20

Just One More Thing...

Steve Jobs

Figure 20.1: The Genius behind all that. Thank you.

And by the way, I bet you didn't know Steve's complete track record. What he did in his lifetime? There might be some things in this list you even did not know:

- worked on Pong at Atari: the first computer game

- Apple I & II: the first personal computers

- Mac: the first PC with a graphical user interface

- NeXT: the computer the World Wide Web was conceived on

- NeXTstep: the worlds most advanced OS that was supposed to shape the future – and did because it became OS-X and iOS (and TV-OS and Watch-OS)

- Toy Story: the first fully computer animated movie

- iPod: the most elegant and usable (mp3) music player

- iTunes: the worlds first working Online Music Store

- OS-X: the Next Generation Mac

- iPhone: the worlds first real smartphone

- iCloud: the only widely user accepted Cloud plattform

- iPad: the worlds first real tablet computer

And these are only the real big ones. Imagine what else he would have done, if he didn't have to leave so early. But geniuses are sometimes just for a while here for us to appreciate them.

The best feature on the the Mac is of course the "I'm a Mac - and I'm a PC" commercials. Have a look at them, if you like. They are funny and say the truth at the same time: Youtube (click here)

All products mentioned in this book are listed on our website at: Think-ebook.com/mac

Index

App Store, 65
Autosave, 72

Backup, 52

Clipboard, 109
Cloud Storage, 63
Copy&Paste, 97

Desktop Search, 48
Dictation, 80
Dock, 36

eMail Attachments, 88
Expose, 44

Finder Tags, 84
Fusion Drive, 78

Harddisk, 78

iCloud, 63
iCloud Drive, 92
iPhone Calls, 89

Launchpad, 68

Maildrop, 88

Model-View-Controller, 34
Multi Touch, 75

Notes App, 69

Optimized Storage, 98

Power Nap, 79
Preview, 58
Program Manager, 68

Quick View, 58
Quicktime, 59

Save Dialog, 109
Siri, 96
Software, 65
Spaces, 54
Speech-to-Text, 80
Spotlight, 48
SSD, 78

Task Overview, 44
Telefone, 89
Text-to-Speech, 81
Time Machine, 52
Trashcan, 109

Universal Clipboard, 97
Unix, 32

Versions, 72

Video Player, 59
Video Recorder, 59
Virtual Desktops, 54

Chapter 21

Recommendations

We of course would also recommend to you the following ebooks...

Luxury Watches – A Purchasing Guide

A luxury watch is more than $5,000. So naturally in this topic there is a lot of money involved. This book will help you to avoid wrong decisions that would cost you huge amounts of money. It will help you to understand how the luxury watch market works. There are a lot of watchmakers and even more watches on the market. It will help you to identify the top brands and watches that not only look nice, but are a good investment into the future. Vintages models are very en vogue for some years now. So if you consider purchasing a luxury watch, there are a lot of things you need to know. Like e.g. What is a luxury watch and what makes it so expensive? What models and brands keep their value over years, which even grow in value? What are the top watch brands of the world? What are the top watch models, the timeless classics available? Should I buy a replica watch? Can a luxury watch be a financial investment like artworks, oldtimers or precious metals? This book will help you with basic knowledge and some personal advice.

Links to all ebooks online stores can also be found on our website at

http://think-ebooks.com/luxury-watches

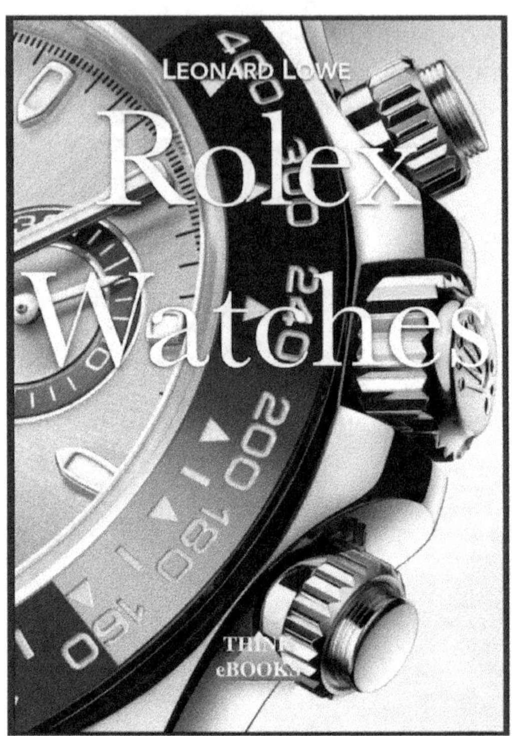

Rolex Watches

5/5 Stars ***** Well worth reading and at a fair price: »This is a very useful and clearly written primer for anyone who is interested in Rolex watches. All of the modern and many of the vintage watches are covered. The compact format is a handy feature.« (Harrell, March 4. 2017)

5/5 Stars ***** MUY BUENO.« (Juan Carlos Camino, March 15. 2017)

This ebook provides a lot of purchase relevant background information on the most important Rolex models. With this ebook you will be able to select the watch you want to purchase with ease. You will have a quick overview of the Rolex models and understand why they are there and why some models are considered more important and valuable than others.

The Rolex lineup of watches evolved over time. And like every naturally evolving structure it is a bit confusing at the first and often also second look. It helps a lot to understand when and why which model was introduced and what changes it got over time. You also will be able to understand the Rolex vintage collectors' movement, that values old Rolex models much higher than the modern lineup.

This ebook tries to sort this out a bit. To understand what watch is meant for what audience, what differences are there between the models, and how the whole thing did evolve since the 1950s, this book will give you some important advice.

It is no question if you will find the best watch for you within the Rolex world, if you just know the details we present to you in this ebook. And selecting the right Rolex is always a matter of money. So be wise and learn, before you buy.

This is not a Rolex sales catalogue. In contrary to such an approach we tried to cover all the information that is not given on official websites but nevertheless should make it much clearer, how the Rolex models are connected to each other and what might be the right one for your wrist.

Links to all ebooks online stores can also be found on our website at

http://think-ebooks.com/rolex-watches

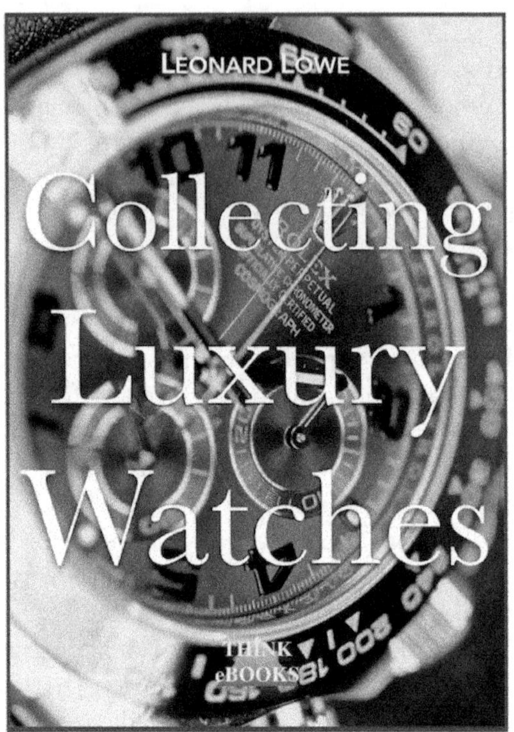

Collecting Luxury Watches

5/5 Stars ***** Great book for watch enthusiasts! This is the second e-book from this author, that I've read. He has a nice, clear writing style and definitely he has lots of insight on what makes a particular watch brand and watch model valuable. I thought the omission of Grand Seiko was somewhat odd, but it is still a great book.« (July 18, 2017)

Leonard Lowe wrote three books about luxury watches: Luxury Watches, Rolex Watches and Ten Fun Things to do with Luxury Watches. And here is his fourth one, his most personal one, with the most insight in his own personal collection and his thoughts why and when he purchased his collectibles. A personal history of becoming a watch enthusiast despite starting out an ordinary person with a lot of hints and thoughts on purchasing and collecting luxury watches.

»I never decided to be a watch collector. It just happened somehow. This book finally tells the story of my passion for luxury watches, how I learned about them, what I considered before and after purchasing my pieces and how it is owning and wearing them. I am sure a lot of my considerations will help the new and even the advanced watch lover to learn even more about watches, about collecting them or – if you're not a collector – just about finding the right one-and-only watch for your wrist. What you will find in this ebook is an amusing, entertaining and insightful story of my personal experiences with luxury watches. Have fun...!«

Join Leonard Lowe on his journey through the world of luxury watches and find a lot of useful and inspiring insights about this compelling hobby.

Links to all ebooks online stores can also be found on our website at

http://think-ebooks.com/collecting-luxury-watches

Ten fun Things to do with Luxury Watches

A book not only about collecting watches...

Ten fun things you can do with luxury watches... well, ok, it ended up being thirteen things, not ten. But that already says a lot. And no, it not only says that you get 30% more than you payed for... it says something about watches, about having watches as a hobby and about the fun you can have with them. Because basically it is always fun to deal with something beautiful, with something perfectionistic and with some piece of art. It means dealing with something higher than you are and that alone lifts you up.

A luxury watch is not just a watch. You can do a lot of smart, fun and interesting things with a watch, inspired by a watch or in companianship with a watch.

This ebook will give you some ideas, inspiration and even reason, why some people are interested in these very special watches and often frantically collect them. Keep in mind: we are talking about watches that are 'defined' by these peculiar characteristics: they are made in Switzerland and they are at least $5000.

Of course there is more to a 'real' luxury watch than these two base characteristics. A lot of people narrow the whole industry that consists of dozens of companies down to about 9 really important companies: Rolex, Omega, Breitling (that much about the companies you probably already heard about) and there is Patek-Philippe, Audemars Piguet and Vacheron Constantain, who are called the Holy Trinity (!) and there is Jaeger-LeCoultre, Breguet and IWC, who are... well... also very important. For a first take you can ignore all the others. Perhaps you will encounter Hublot and Panerai and other brands that try to distinguish themselves from the mainstream. They can be entertaining too...

Watches are a really rewarding hobby. You can do a lot of things with watches and around them. They are a kind of technology that is around for about 300 years and the oldest companies in the market are nearly there from the very beginning. So you can learn a lot about very different areas on this very peculiar, very special and very secluded market: about luxury of course, also about style, about beauty, about technology, about marketing, about riches and rich people, about capital, money and lasting value, about time and timelessness, about fun and application, about diving, space travel, precision measurement and last but not least about the biggest secret of them all: about time.

So let's have a little stroll around and look what watches have got in for you. There is something that you will find interesting or even inspiring. Trust me and come with me for a few precious moments together...

Links to all ebooks online stores can also be found on our website at

http://think-ebooks.com/ten-fun-things-to-do-with-luxury-watches/

The ONE Solution

In science and in R&D you always, over and over, are facing the same kind of questions: how does this work? How can we make that better? There are subtle variations but the basic idea is always the same. How can we get this thing going, and why.

And there is a solution to that problem! There is a method, a way to solve all of these problems.

But despite the fact that it is the same question all the time, researchers and scientists all over the world keep, from a methodological standpoint *doing it wrong*. And that is why developer and even scientists do worse than they could do.

The cause often might be that they are very much focused on their content and not very much on their methods. Methods are widely ignored in Universities all over the world in favor of the knowledge of facts.

But that is a mistake. Methods are 'how to do something', 'how to reach goals'. So they are obviously most important. And by ignoring that they use methods at all and that there are better ones around that really do work, researchers keep using the most basic and most simple and most *wrong* method they can possibly use. Simply because it's the only one they know, because they never thought about their work that way.

And the result is always the same: R&D seems a pretty hard thing to do. Consuming a lot of time, immense costs and with unclear results. Because of that, R&D is even often done in the most imperfect way you can imagine just to keep costs down.

You don't believe me? Well, give it a shot. I met so many researchers in small and large companies, at universities and in applied science who all did the same thing *wrong* and who all in the same way marveled about their poor results!

This book is about methods, about One method, that has the power to solve most of the problems in R&D and science in 30% of the time with 30% of the costs. And it solves *every problem*, even those who seem insoluble to even the best researchers out there.

That is the power of this method I will describe. It has been used for more than ten years now, it has been proven, it is also used by top companies already. But still many researchers use their old, their *wrong* method and do not meet their goals as they could, if they'd put more attention to the method they use.

Here is how you can work the most efficient way.

Links to all ebooks online stores can also be found on our website at

http://think-ebooks.com/the-one-solution

Tell us Your Opinion

Thank you very much for reading this ebook. We would of course very much appreciate if you liked the ebook. If you have any further questions on the subject, have some criticism or ideas for improvement please feel free to tell us your thoughts: please write to leo.lowe@rocketmail.com or visit our website at THINK-ebooks.com